SUPER IQ TESTS

Fraser Simpson

PUZZLE
WRIGHT
PRESS

New York

PUZZLE
WRIGHT
PRESS

New York

An Imprint of Sterling Publishing
387 Park Avenue South
New York, NY 10016

PUZZLEWRIGHT PRESS and the distinctive Puzzlewright Press logo are registered trademarks of Sterling Publishing Co., Inc.

© 2012 by Fraser Simpson
Original edition © 2000 by Fraser Simpson
Illustrations by Myron Miller

ISBN 978-1-4027-9727-9

Distributed in Canada by Sterling Publishing
℅ Canadian Manda Group, 165 Dufferin Street
Toronto, Ontario, Canada M6K 3H6
Distributed in the United Kingdom by GMC Distribution Services
Castle Place, 166 High Street, Lewes, East Sussex, England BN7 1XU
Distributed in Australia by Capricorn Link (Australia) Pty. Ltd.
P.O. Box 704, Windsor, NSW 2756, Australia

For information about custom editions, special sales, and premium and corporate purchases, please contact Sterling Special Sales at 800-805-5489 or specialsales@sterlingpublishing.com.

Manufactured in China

2 4 6 8 10 9 7 5 3 1

www.puzzlewright.com

CONTENTS

Introduction **4**

Test 1 .... **6**
    Answers...**14**

Test 2 ....**18**
    Answers...**26**

Test 3 ....**30**
    Answers...**36**

Test 4 ....**40**
    Answers...**46**

Test 5 ....**50**
    Answers...**56**

Test 6 ....**60**
    Answers...**66**

Test 7 ....**70**
    Answers...**76**

Test 8 ....**80**
    Answers...**86**

Test 9 ....**90**
    Answers...**96**

Test 10 .... **100**
    Answers...**108**

Test 11 .... **112**
    Answers...**118**

Test 12 .... **122**
    Answers...**128**

Test 13 .... **132**
    Answers...**138**

Test 14 .... **142**
    Answers...**150**

Test 15 .... **154**
    Answers...**160**

Test 16 .... **164**
    Answers...**170**

Test 17 .... **174**
    Answers...**180**

Test 18 .... **184**
    Answers...**192**

Test 19 .... **196**
    Answers...**202**

Test 20 .... **206**
    Answers...**214**

Test 21 .... **218**
    Answers...**226**

Test 22 .... **230**
    Answers...**237**

INTRODUCTION

Books with "IQ Test" in the title generally contain a mishmash of number, word, and logic puzzles, sometimes with time limits, and usually divided into several tests. Often, there's a scoring system. And sometimes there's an earnest introduction discussing intelligence quotient and official testing procedures and why you shouldn't feel bad about yourself if you happen to do poorly on such tests.

This book is no different, except for the earnest introduction. If you're the puzzle type, I hope you'll find lots here to keep you entertained, including traditional IQ-book fare as well other puzzle types. Every test has 15 questions, and if you want to use a time limit, give yourself exactly 45 minutes for each test. If that doesn't work, try 60 minutes per test. For a scoring system, you can use this sharpness chart:

15	Razor-sharp
13–14	Sharp as a tack
10–12	Serrated edge
7–9	Butter knife
0–6	Needs stropping

This book's format has each test laid out on four or six pages, followed directly by the answers to the test (except for Test 22, which, due to large illustrations and diagrams, runs seven pages). This way, you don't have to flip to the back of the book after finishing a test to find the solutions. The tests aren't intended to get any harder or easier as you go through the book, but you'll probably discover that you'll get the hang of some of the repeated puzzle types as you go through. This may make your solving faster.

Time yourself if you're so inclined, or work through the tests in a leisurely fashion. However you decide, happy puzzling!

—Fraser Simpson

1. Match each picture in the top row with a picture in the bottom row by writing letters in the blanks.

A

B

C

D

___

___

___

___

2. Which of A, B, C, or D has the unusual property shared by the six words in the first column?

MESDAMES   A. RESTORES
BLEACHABLE   B. DEIFIED
HOTSHOT   C. OVERDONE
TORMENTOR   D. PHOTOGRAPH
UNDERFUND
ANTIPERSPIRANT

3. In each row of this chart, the third number is formed from the first two using the same arithmetic pattern. What number completes the last row?

5	1	24
8	10	54
3	2	7
2	3	1
7	9	40
10	2	

4. Remove six toothpicks and leave two squares.

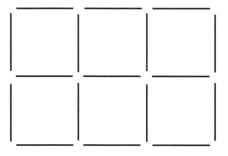

5. Think of a word that fits in the first blank, and remove the first three letters to form the word for the second blank. What are the two words?

Feeling a bit _____ after the revolving fairground ride, I decided to remain _____ on the bench while the others went on the ride a second time.

6. Find the value of ☐.

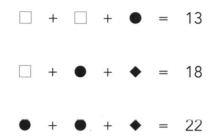

☐ + ☐ + ● = 13

☐ + ● + ◆ = 18

● + ● + ◆ = 22

7. What part of the body can be inserted into each of these to make three words?

CELIER

SY

MERCISE

8. What seven-letter vegetable can be made solely from the seven letters that represent musical notes? Some letters may be repeated.

A B C D E F G

9. Which is the odd one out?

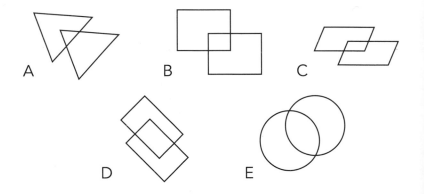

A   B   C

D   E

10. Fill in a letter to complete a word. Figuring out which way the word reads (clockwise or counterclockwise) is part of the challenge. What is the word?

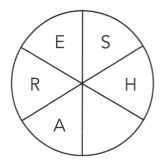

11. If today is Tuesday, what day of the week is three days after four days before the day after tomorrow?

12. What are the next two terms in this sequence?

B   19   D   17   F   14   H   10   J   ___   ___

13. A four-digit number multiplied by a one-digit number yields another four-digit number, and all nine digits from 1 to 9 appear in the multiplication. Fill in the digits 3, 6, 7, 8, and 9 in two different ways below to make a correct answer to this problem. Above each problem, we've provided a handy cross-off chart of the digits to use.

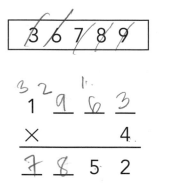

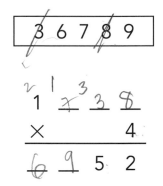

14. In how many different ways can you make change for $3.00, using combinations of only dimes and/or nickels?

15. What word meaning "a shout of derision" can be represented by NEWNESS in a cryptogram?

1. BDAC
    Pictures represent anagram pairs. Rearrange the
    word representing one picture to get the word
    representing its mate. The pairs are:
        HOSE & SHOE
        COAT & TACO
        PALM & LAMP
        MOAT & ATOM

2. A. RESTORES
    The first three letters and last three letters of each
    word are the same.

3. 98
    In each row, square the first number and then
    subtract the second number. The calculation for the
    last row is $(10 \times 10) - 2 = 98$.

4. Here is one way to accomplish the feat:

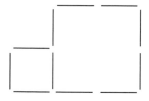

5. NAUSEATED, SEATED

6. $\square$ = 3

Add the first two rows together. The sum is:
$$\square + \square + \square + \bullet + \bullet + \blacklozenge = 31$$
Subtract off the third row, which is:
$$\bullet + \bullet + \blacklozenge = 22$$
The result is: $\square + \square + \square = 9$. Since 3 $\square$'s total 9, each $\square$ is worth 3. Alternately, since $\square + \square + \bullet = 13$, the value of $\square$ must be small. Try the values $\square = 1$, $\square = 2$, $\square = 3$, etc. until the equations work.

7. HAND

The words formed are CHANDELIER, SHANDY, and MERCHANDISE.

8. CABBAGE

9. E

In all of the other pairs, the overlapping part looks the same as the original shapes.

10. SERAPH

Fill in a P and read counterclockwise from the S.

11. Wednesday

You could work backward, but you don't have to. Instead, do this to calculate the shift:

"three days after" = plus 3
"four days before" = minus 4
"the day after tomorrow" = plus 2

The shift resolves to $3 - 4 + 2 = 1$.
One day after Tuesday is Wednesday.

12. 5 and L

Two sequences are nested. The letters move two forward in the alphabet, while the numbers decrease by one more each time.

13. 1738 × 4 = 6952 and 1963 × 4 = 7852

14. 31 ways

Ignore the nickels. You can use any amount of dimes from 0 dimes to 30 dimes, filling in the remaining amount with nickels. This makes 31 different combinations in all.

15. CATCALL

The word CATCALL has the same letter-substitution pattern as NEWNESS.

1. The numbers in the diagrams combine in the same way to make correct arithmetic statements. What number is missing from the last diagram?

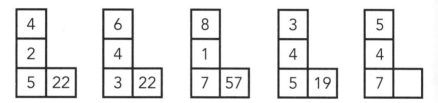

2. I'm thinking of a number. I multiply it by 3, then subtract 6, then divide by 9, then add 5. The final result is 7. What was my original number?

3. The word "flighty," written in lower case on lined paper, has all of its letters projecting either above or below the line (the g hangs down, the i has a dot above, etc.). What eleven-letter word meaning "butterflies in the stomach" has no letters projecting above or below the line?

4. Which of A, B, C, or D has the unusual property shared by the six words in the first column?

MILLION

CANAPE

COMMANDEER

SHARE

VAMOOSE

KAYAK

A. GLOBETROTTER

B. TRIGGER

C. CREOSOTE

D. JACKET

5. Hidden in the grid are 5 five-letter words in a continuous closed path that does not cross itself. Go from letter to letter horizontally, vertically, or diagonally. What are the five words?

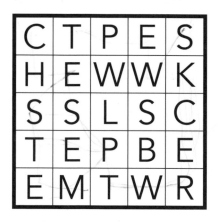

C	T	P	E	S
H	E	W	W	K
S	S	L	S	C
T	E	P	B	E
E	M	T	W	R

_____

_____

_____

_____

_____

6. Fill in the blanks to make two words meaning "fate" or "destiny."

K __ __ M __   K __ __ M __ __

7. TESTED is to DETEST as 654321 is to _____.

   A. 123456
   B. 126534
   C. 125643
   D. 153264
   E. 156243

8. The digit-sum of the three-digit number 285 is 15, because 2 + 8 + 5 = 15. How many three-digit numbers have a digit-sum of 25 or greater?

9. Fill in the next domino in this sequence:

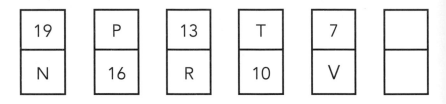

19	P	13	T	7	
N	16	R	10	V	

10. Change one letter in each word below to make a new word. The five new letters, in order, form a word. What is this five-letter word?

PROPANE
REDNESS
IMPRESS
REVERIE
NOUGAT

11. Make 4 eight-letter words by joining these four-letter words in pairs. (For example, THIN + KING gives THINKING.)

BORN
DISC
FEAT
HERS
OVER
PEAR
REAP
STUB

12. What is the next term in this sequence?

4 7 13 25 49 97 193 ____

13. Put the nine words, crossword-style, into this 5×5 grid. The shaded region will spell a five-letter word that does not appear in the word list. What is this word?

ALICE PLACE STEER
ASIAN RESET WHAMS
MECCA SONAR WRAPS

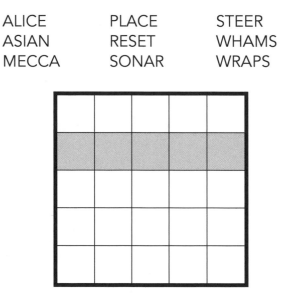

14. Change one letter in each word to form a common saying.

COED HANGS, WARY HEARD.

15. STRESSES is to TREE as STUTTGART is to
_____.

1. 39

    In each diagram, multiply the top and bottom numbers of the left-hand column and add the middle one to form the number at the bottom right. The calculation for the last diagram is
    $(5 \times 7) + 4 = 39$.

2. 8

    Working backward, $7 - 5 = 2$, then $2 \times 9 = 18$, then $18 + 6 = 24$, then $24 \div 3 = 8$.

3.

    # nervousness

    A list of lower-case nonprojecting letters (letters without ascenders or descenders) is: a, c, e, m, n, o, r, s, u, v, w, x, z.

4. A. GLOBETROTTER
    Each word ends with the name of an animal: LION, APE, DEER, HARE, MOOSE, YAK, OTTER.

5. SWEPT, CHEWS, BLESS, TEMPT, WRECK
Each of these words is a five-letter word with E as its only vowel.

6. KARMA and KISMET
"Karma" is from Sanskrit and "kismet" is from Arabic.

7. E
Write TESTED above 654321 and you have the substitutions 6 = T, 5 = E, 4 = S, 3 = T, 2 = E, 1 = D. Encoding the answers in order gives: DETSET, DETETS, DEETST, DETETS, DETEST. The last one, letter E, is correct.

8. 10 numbers

The secret is to list them in an organized way.

Digit-sum of 27: 999

Digit-sum of 26: 998, 989, 899

Digit-sum of 25: 988, 898, 889, 997, 979, 799

9.

X
4

In the zigzag letter pattern, the letters continually move forward by two, whereas in the zigzag number pattern, the numbers continually decrease by three.

10. FRESH

The new words are proFane, redRess, Empress, reverSe, and nougHt.

11. DISCOVER, FEATHERS, REAPPEAR, STUBBORN

12. 385

One way of looking at the pattern is that each term is twice the previous term, minus one. Thus the calculation for the final term is $(2 \times 193) - 1 = 385$. A second method is to keep adding terms of the doubling sequence 3, 6, 12, 24, 48, 96, 192. The calculation for the final term is then $193 + 192 = 385$.

13. HELLO

The bottom row must contain a word consisting of the final letters of five other words in the list. This can only be STEER or RESET. Since only ALICE and PLACE end with the letter E, the letter pattern of the top row must be ??AP?, ??PA?, ?A?P?, or ?P?A?. The only word in the list that fits any of these patterns is WRAPS. The completed grid looks like this:

14. Cold hands, warm heart.

15. SUGAR

Remove the letter that appears four times in each case. Removing four S's from STRESSES leaves TREE. Similarly, removing four T's from STUTTGART leaves SUGAR.

TEST 3

1. Replace the blanks in each of these words with four consecutive letters of the alphabet, in order. For example, given "___ I ___ ___ T ___ N G," you would place the consecutive letters FGHI in the blanks to spell FIGHTING.

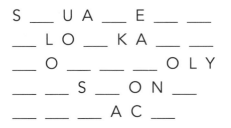

S ___ U A ___ E ___ ___

___ L O ___ K A ___ ___

___ O ___ ___ ___ O L Y

___ ___ S ___ O N ___

___ ___ ___ A C ___

2. What seven-letter word is something you can charge—or get charged with?

3. What identical three-letter word can precede all five words to form five new words?

_ _ _ PEST   _ _ _ SON

_ _ _ ASK   _ _ _ AGE

_ _ _ NATION

4. Rhyme time! If a house pet with the gift of gab is a VERBAL GERBIL, what is a tulip or rose with a lemony taste?

5. If the first two statements of this syllogism are true, is the conclusion true, false, or uncertain?

All good house pets are clean.
My gerbil is clean.
Conclusion: My gerbil is a good house pet.

6. Find two different ways to place four more chess queens on squares of this 5×5 grid so that no two attack each other. (That is, no two queens may lie on the same column, row, or diagonal.)

7. Fill in the missing number.

CIVIC = 207
MIX = 1011
LIVID = 557
MILD = _____

8. Complete these seven-letter words. Put one letter in each blank.

```
___  A  T  H  T  U  ___
___  R  E  G  A  N  ___
___  N  T  A  R  I  ___
___  I  N  F  O  L  ___
___  D  U  C  A  T  ___
___  E  W  B  O  R  ___
___  I  A  M  O  N  ___
___  U  C  C  E  S  ___
```

9. What four-letter word completes this analogy?

PULP is to PUMP as BURY is to _____.

10. If XPDNC is "expediency," what eight-letter word is NCQR?

11. What are the next two terms in this sequence?

132 44 51 17 24 8 15 5 ____ ____

12. Change one letter in each of these words to make a familiar threesome:

TIN   PLATE   CHOW

13. The numbers in the diagrams combine in the same way to make correct arithmetic statements. What number is missing from the last diagram?

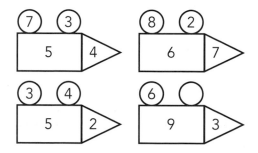

14. Which of A, B, C, or D has the unusual property shared by the six words in the first column?

APPEAR
DETAIN
FORMAT
JOVIAN
KENNED
SQUEAK

A. CURFEW
B. GRATIS
C. LESSON
D. PISTON

15. How many triangles of all sizes are there in this diagram?

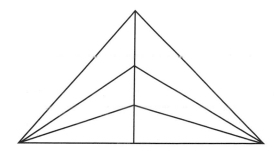

1. SQUAREST
   BLOCKADE
   MONOPOLY
   ABSCOND
   HIJACK

2. BATTERY
   You can charge a battery cell, or you can get charged with (assault and) battery.

3. DAM
   The words formed are DAMPEST, DAMASK, DAMNATION, DAMSON, and DAMAGE.

4. SOUR FLOWER

5. Uncertain
   The conclusion would be true had the first statement said "All clean things are good house pets." The given statements provide no information about bad house pets; so, for all we know, some clean things may also be bad house pets.

6.

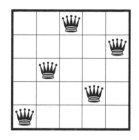 and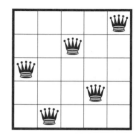

A good way to start this problem is by shading in all of the squares where you cannot place a queen because it would be attacked by the original queen, as shown at right. One of the two unshaded squares in the upper right-hand column must contain a queen; try each one to get the two solutions.

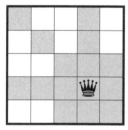

7. 1551

Each word is worth the sum of its letters taken as Roman numerals (I = 1, V = 5, X = 10, L = 50, C = 100, D = 500, and M = 1000). Therefore, MILD = 1000 + 1 + 50 + 500.

8. BATHTUB
   OREGANO
   ONTARIO
   KINFOLK
   EDUCATE
   NEWBORN
   DIAMOND
   SUCCESS
   The right and left columns spell "BOOKENDS."

9. BUSY
   Move the third letter one place forward in the alphabet. Moving L to M makes PULP into PUMP. Similarly, moving R to S makes BURY into BUSY.

10. INSECURE
    NCQR sounds somewhat like "insecure" when you say the letters out loud.

11. 12 and 4
    The sequence alternates: divide by 3, add 7, divide by 3, add 7.

12. WIN, PLACE, SHOW

13. 5

Add the numbers in the left circle and the rectangle, and then divide by the number in the triangle. The calculation for the final answer is $(6 + 9) \div 3 = 5$.

14. D. PISTON

All the words become new words when their last letter is changed to L. Those new words are APPEAL, DETAIL, FORMAL, JOVIAL, KENNEL, SQUEAL, and PISTOL.

15. 15 triangles

Here is a list, using the labeled diagram.
One piece: A, B, C, D, E, F
Two pieces: AC, CE, BD, DF, EF
Three pieces: ACE, BDF
Four pieces: CDEF
Six pieces: ABCDEF

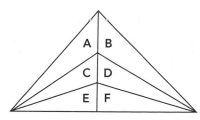

1. Complete this analogy:

   HEIGHT is to EIGHTH as SCARES is to

   _____.

2. In the fifth diagram of this sequence, 11 squares should be shaded and 4 left unshaded. Fill in the pattern for the fifth diagram.

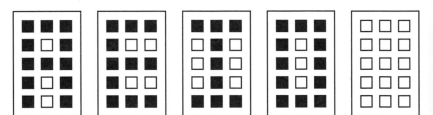

3. Match each picture in the top row with a picture in the bottom row by writing letters in the blanks.

A   B   C   D

___   ___   ___   ___

4. In a herd of cows, there are 84 more legs than eyes. How many cows are in the herd?

5. Insert a six-letter animal, one letter per square, across the bottom row of this grid so that six common three-letter words are formed reading down.

6. What are the next two terms in this mathematical sequence?

1 2 4 6 10 12 16 18 22 ____ ____

7. Wht ght-lttr wrd mnng "pwr" r "mght" hs nly n vwl?

8. Which of A, B, C, or D has the unusual property shared by the six words in the first column?

DALHOUSIE   A. CAUTIONARY
EDUCATION   B. PNEUMONIA
DIALOGUE   C. HOUSECOAT
MIAOUED   D. BUOYANT
MENDACIOUS
EUPHORIA

9. Two of these proverbs have practically opposite meanings. Which two?

A. Better safe than sorry.
B. Look before you leap.
C. Where there's a will, there's a way.
D. Attack is the best form of defense.
E. Nothing ventured, nothing gained.

10. On a clock, what is the ratio of the speed of the hour hand to the speed of the minute hand?

11. Fill in a letter to complete a word reading clockwise or counterclockwise. What is the word?

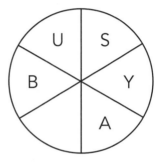

12. In a group of five people, everyone shakes hands once with everyone else. How many handshakes take place?

13. What do pianos, janitors, typewriters, Florida, and basketball courts have in common?

14. Give the two common four-letter words that can be formed by rearranging the main compass points: N, W, S, E.

15. Which of A, B, C, or D comes next in this sequence?

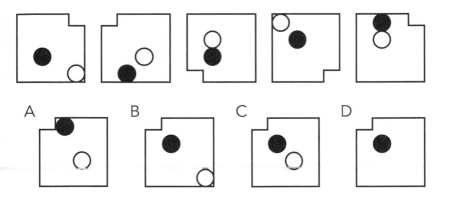

A   B   C   D

1. CARESS
   Move the first letter to the end of the word. Moving the H at the front of HEIGHT to the end spells EIGHTH. Similarly, moving the S at the front of SCARES to the end spells CARESS.

2. Seen from a distance, the patterns form the vowels A, E, I, O, U.

3. ADBC
   Remove the last letter from each object in the top row to make its match in the bottom row.
   > BEARD & BEAR
   > FORTY & FORT
   > CROWN & CROW
   > PEARL & PEAR

4. 42

There are two "extra" legs for each cow, so there are
84 ÷ 2 = 42 cows.

5. COYOTE

The words formed are TIC, EGO, ANY, BOO, ART,
GEE. One way to solve this is to list the possibilities
for each spot vertically and search for an answer
reading across. Here's the list of possibilities:

6. 28 and 30

The numbers are one less than the primes (2, 3, 5, 7, 11, 13, 17, 19, 23, 29, 31, etc.). A prime number is a number with exactly two factors (itself and 1).

7. STRENGTH (or STRNGTH)

The vowel-less question reads, "What eight-letter word meaning 'power' or 'might' has only one vowel?"

8. B. PNEUMONIA

Each word contains all five vowels (A, E, I, O, U) in some order.

9. A and E

10. 1:12

The minute hand moves 12 times as fast as the hour hand, traveling around the clock face 12 times in the time it takes the hour hand to go around once.

11. SUBWAY

Fill in a W and read counterclockwise from the S.

12. 10 handshakes
   Method 1
   If each of the 5 people shakes hands with each of the other 4, this gives $5 \times 4 = 20$ handshakes. But this would have each person shaking hands twice (A shakes with B, then later B shakes with A). So there are only $20 \div 2 = 10$ handshakes if everyone shakes once.

   Method 2
   Add $4 + 3 + 2 + 1 = 10$, since each subsequent person shakes hands with one person fewer.

13. They all have KEYS

14. NEWS and SEWN

15. C
   The indentation rotates counterclockwise through the four corners, while the black circle moves up and down and the white circle moves back and forth diagonally.

TEST 5

1. Which anagram is the odd one out?

DITSUP
LETTINGNILE
STARM
THRIBG
VCREEL

2. A theater's admission cost for 2 adults and 3 children is $36. An adult's ticket is three times the cost of a child's ticket. What is the price of admission for a child?

3. Create three 8-letter words by inserting three of these four-letter words in the exact centers of the other three. For example, YALE inside LOST gives LOYALEST.

> ARCH
> GAME
> LATE
> LINT
> SEES
> UREA

4. What two shades of red contain the word CAR?

5. What is the next term in this sequence?

> E1 O2 E3 R4 E5 X6 N7 T8 ____

6. Solve this unusul crossword.

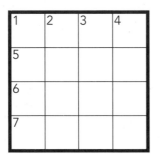

CROSS
1. Crzy nd impulsive
5. Miniture
6. Topek's stte
7. Reson for using n inhler

DOWN
1. Hlloween disguises
2. Unwvering
3. ____ of the Titns
4. Blood prt

7. What African place name of 11 letters contains all of the letters I, J, K, L, M, N, and O?

8. You can change a ROMAN into a ROWAN tree by flipping the M over to change it into a W. What famous inventor is made worse by this process?

9. What do these four things have in common? (For a hint, shift the letters of this phrase ahead 13 letters in the alphabet: "va gur fjvz.")

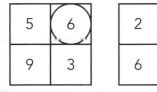

10. The numbers in the diagrams combine in the same way to make correct arithmetic statements. What number is missing from the last diagram?

5	6
9	3

2	8
6	7

11	25
8	3

3	
4	9

11. S **C R** U G **E** A **A** R **M** is "cream" and "sugar" interwoven. Both words keep their correct order reading from left to right. What two "this and that" words are interwoven here?

F I T E R L A C K D

12. How should the final cube be marked in this sequence?

13. Some number of people are spaced equally around the perimeter of a circle and are then numbered consecutively, clockwise, starting from 1. Person number 11 is directly opposite person number 35. How many people are there around the circle?

14. What eight-letter car part becomes an item in a purse when you change its first letter from D to L?

15. Match each picture in the top row with a picture in the bottom row by writing letters in the blanks.

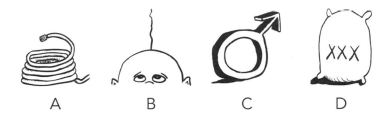

A   B   C   D

1. DITSUP

    The groups of letters can be rearranged to form
    these words: STUPID, INTELLIGENT, SMART, BRIGHT,
    and CLEVER.

2. $4

    The two adults are the same price as 6 children. The
    equivalent of 9 children got in for $36, so each child's
    admission cost is $36 ÷ 9 = $4.

3. LAUREATE, LIGAMENT, SEARCHES

4. CARmine and sCARlet

5. E9

    The terms are numbers preceded by the last
    letters of their names. Since the last letter of the word
    "nine" is E, the solution is E9.

6. The clues suggest leaving out all of the A's. All of the answers to the clues contain only the vowel A. The words across are MADCAP, SMALL, KANSAS, and ASTHMA. The words down are MASKS, ADAMANT, CLASH, and PLASMA.

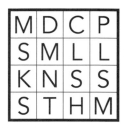

7. KILIMANJARO
   The highest mountain in Africa, Kilimanjaro is found in northeast Tanzania.

8. MORSE
   If you flip the M, then MORSE is made WORSE.

9. The pictures show a sole, perch, skate, and ray. These are all types of fish. (The hint, decoded, reads "in the swim.")

10. 23
   Multiply the upper left and lower right numbers, and then subtract the lower left number. The calculation is $(3 \times 9) - 4 = 23$.

11. TRACK and FIELD

12.

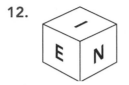

The letters on the cubes, reading clockwise from the top, are the last three letters of the words in the numerical sequence ONE, thREE, fIVE, seVEN, nINE.

13. 48 people

If you subtract the numbers belonging to opposite people on a circle, you always have the same difference. (Think of a clock face; the difference there is always 6.) In this circle, the difference is 35 – 11 = 24, which is halfway around the circle. Therefore there are 24 × 2 = 48 people in all.

14. DIPSTICK

Change the D to L and you have LIPSTICK.

15. CDBA

The pictures represent homophones. HOSE sounds like HOES; HAIR sounds like HARE; MALE sounds like MAIL; and FLOUR sounds like FLOWER.

TEST 6

1. Each of the six letters stands for a different from from 1 through 9. Using the three clues below, can you deduce the number represented by each letter?

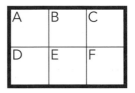

All three columns down total 13.
The value of A + E is 9.
The value of E + F is 12.

2. What noted explorer's name is a rearrangement of LEG HAIR?

3. The numbers in the diagrams combine in the same way to make correct arithmetic statements. What number is missing from the last diagram?

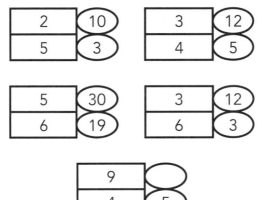

4. What six lottor word roprosonting a group of intelligent primates has its letters in alphabetical order?

A B C D E F G H I J K L M N O P Q R S T U V W X Y Z

5. Each letter has been given a number from 1 to 4. What is the proper encoding for ZENITH?

```
F A M I L Y     H A M L E T
3 3 4 1 2 3     3 3 4 2 4 2

W E A K L Y     Z E N I T H
4 4 3 3 2 3     _ _ _ _ _ _
```

6. What is the next date in this sequence?

January 7, February 8, March 5, April 5, May 3, June 4, July 4, _____

7. A car odometer reads 279972, which is a palindrome (it reads the same forward and backward). What is the next palindrome that will appear on this odometer?

8. Wheel 1 has the letters A, B, C, D, E, F in that order on its six faces. Wheel 2 has the letters P, Q, R, S, T, U in that order on its six faces. Wheel 1 turns clockwise, one position every minute. Wheel 2 turns counterclockwise, two positions every minute. Right now, the letters on the front faces are B and Q. Eight minutes from now, what two letters will be on the front faces?

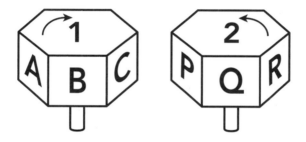

9. Insert a four-letter country into these letters to make a word.

PHA

10. What is the value of this unusual math expression?

(The Beatles) × (Greek muses) ÷
(*Degrees of Separation*) + (Disney dwarfs) −
(legs on a spider)

11. What is the next term in this sequence?

2   5   7   12   19   31   50   81   131   _____

12. Think of a word that fits in the first blank, and add two letters in front to form the word for the second blank. What are the two words?

Most _____ car agencies will not allow a teenager as a driver, even if Mom or Dad is willing to sign a form indicating _____ permission.

13. Which is the odd one out?

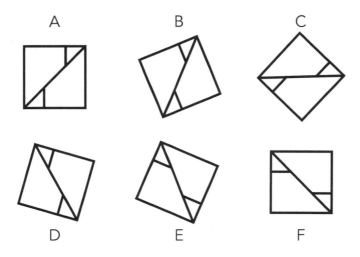

A   B   C

D   E   F

14. What insect becomes a snake when you cut off its head?

15. Sam is 4 years younger than Paula. In 8 years, Paula will be 35. How old was Sam two years ago?

ANSWERS 6

1.

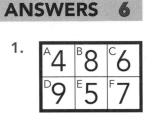

There are only three combinations of two numbers that total 13: (9,4), (8,5), (7,6), so the grid contains no numbers smaller than 4. If A + E = 9, then A and E must be 4 and 5 in some order. Since E + F = 12, we have E and F restricted to 5 and 7 in some order. The overlapping letter is E, so E = 5. Continue filling in the grid using the other restrictions.

2. (Sir Walter) RALEIGH

3. 18

Add the numbers in the two rectangles and the lower circle to get the number in the upper circle. The calculation for the answer is 9 + 4 + 5 = 18.

4. CHIMPS

5. ZENITH is 343123
   Each letter is represented by the number of strokes
   needed to write it.

6. August 6
   Each month is followed by the number of letters in
   the month's name. Since August has six letters, the
   answer is August 6.

7. 280082
   If we can keep the 2 at the beginning, we should. If
   we can keep the 27 at the beginning, we should.
   But we can't, since the middle numbers are both 9's.
   So we move up to 2 8 _ _ 8 2. The smallest numbers
   that can go in the blanks are zeros.

8. D and S
   The sequence of front faces by the minutes is:

Minute:	1	2	3	4	5	6	7	8
Wheel 1:	C	D	E	F	A	B	C	D
Wheel 2:	U	S	Q	U	S	Q	U	S

9. PIRANHA

Insert the country IRAN.

10. 5

The Beatles = 4
Greek muses = 9
Degrees of Separation = 6
Disney dwarfs = 7
Legs on a spider = 8
The calculation is $4 \times 9 \div 6 + 7 - 8 = 5$.

11. 212

Each number is the sum of the two before it. The calculation for the answer is $81 + 131 = 212$.

12. RENTAL, PARENTAL

13. D

All of the other shapes are identical when rotated.

14. WASP

WASP becomes ASP when you "cut off its head," i.e., remove its first letter.

15. 21

Paula is 35 − 8 = 27 now, so Sam is 27 − 4 = 23 now. Two years ago, Sam was 23 − 2 = 21 years old.

TEST 7

1. ASTONISH is an eight-letter word beginning with ASTO. Give a seven-letter synonym for "astonish" that begins with the same four letters.

2. Which of A, B, or C comes next in this sequence?

A   B   C

3. What do a symphony, a train, and lightning hitting earth all have in common?

4. Two numbers add up to 6 and have a difference of 6. What are the numbers?

5. A six-letter word meaning "item of apparel" becomes a six-letter word meaning "*items* of apparel" when you change its only vowel from an O to an I. What are the two words?

6. Fill in a letter to complete a word reading clockwise or counterclockwise. What is the word?

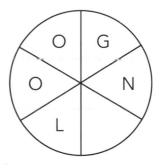

7. What is the next term in this sequence?

1 2 4 8 1 6 3 2 6 4 1 2 ____

8. A discount chain wants the phone number (949) 729-6673 because of a 10-letter message that the number spells. What's the message?

9. Find the six-letter word that finishes this analogy:

CREATION is to RAIN as INDISCREETLY is to

_____.

10. Study these playing cards to figure out our encoding scheme.

A to H:

I to L:

M to Q:

R to Z:

Now decode the five-letter word represented by these cards:

11. Calculate the final result of this series:

$$100 - 98 + 96 - 94 + 92 - 90 + \ldots + 8 - 6 + 4 - 2$$

12. Four related five-letter words are hidden below. The hidden words are spelled out, top to bottom, using one letter from each word. You can cross off a letter as you use it, since no letter is used more than once. What are the four words? (Remember: the words you find will be related.)

```
L  O  C  H
A  L  T  O
T  R  A  M
S  E  E  M
R  E  A  L
```

13. What familiar foursome is this?

THORN SHOUT STEW SATE

14. What eight-letter word meaning "alarmed" is made up of a word meaning "go first" followed by a word meaning "went first"?

15. In each line, find a four-letter word that follows the first word and precedes the second word to form two phrases. (For example, MATCH ___ BLANK makes "match point" and "point blank" when POINT is entered.) The three words you supply, in order, will form a familiar phrase.

HOG	_____	CARD
MAE	_____	POINT
PUPPET	_____	BUSINESS

1. ASTOUND

2. C
   The entire pattern rotates 90° clockwise at each step.

3. A conductor
   A symphony is led by a conductor, a train has a conductor who collects tickets, and the earth serves as a conductor for the lightning.

4. 6 and 0

5. SHORTS and SHIRTS

6. OOLONG (tea)

7. 8
   Mentally respace the numbers in the sequence this way: 1 2 4 8 16 32 64 12_. These numbers are the powers of 2, and the last one should be 128, so the missing number is 8.

8. WHY PAY MORE?

The message is spelled by the associated letters on a telephone keypad. One way to solve this is to list the possibilities for each number vertically and look for the answer reading across.

```
9  4  9  7  2  9  6  6  7  3
W  G  W  P  A  W  M  M  P  D
X  H  X  R  B  X  N  N  R  E
Y  I  Y  S  C  Y  O  O  S  F
```

9. NICETY

The word RAIN is found by reading every second letter in the word CREATION. The word found by taking the letters in the even-numbered positions of the word INDISCREETLY is NICETY.

10. POKER

A to H beside the 8 of spades means that the eight letters A, B, C, D, E, F, G, H are represented in the code by the first eight spades (Ace, 2, 3, 4, 5, 6, 7, 8), respectively. Similarly, I, J, K, and L are represented by the first four diamonds; M, N, O, P, and Q are represented by the first five clubs; and R, S, T, U, V, W, X, Y, and Z are represented by the first nine hearts. So we can now decode the five-letter word:

The fourth "clubs" letter is P.
The third "clubs" letter is O.
The third "diamonds" letter is K.
The fourth "spades" letter is E.
The first "hearts" letter is R.

11. 50

Group the numbers in pairs, like this: (100 – 98) + (96 – 94) + . . . + (8 – 6) + (4 – 2). There are 25 bracketed pairs, because the first numbers in the pairs are the multiples of 4, and 100 ÷ 4 = 25. Since there are 25 pairs, and each has a value of 2, the calculation comes out to 25 × 2 = 50.

12. LLAMA, OTTER, CAMEL, and HORSE
For example, LLAMA is found by taking the L of LOCH, the L of ALTO, the A of TRAM, the M of SEEM, and the A of REAL.

13. Anagrams of NORTH, SOUTH, WEST and EAST

14. STARTLED
The word is START followed by LED.

15. WILD WEST SHOW
WILD makes the phrases "hog wild" and "wild card." WEST makes "Mae West" and "West Point." SHOW makes "puppet show" and "show business."

TEST 8

1. An anagram of PER YARD is something that might be priced per yard. What is it?

2. Which of A, B, C, or D has the unusual property shared by the six words in the first column?

SHED   A. DONUT
WERE   B. YOUNG
ILL   C. WELL
CANT   D. HERE
HELL
ID

3. What four-letter word can be put in both blanks to create two new words?

PA _____ T   VI _____ L

4. A word for a person who raises fruits and vegetables becomes a word for a person who sells fruits and vegetables when you change its fourth letter from a W to a C. What are the two words?

5. Although this is not a regular cryptogram, each letter must be replaced with a different letter using some method. All of the punctuation is correct. What's the (music-related) message?

K'K   CL   CA/FA   HYP.

6. If today is Wednesday, what day of the week will it be 65 days from today?

7. There are 360° in a full circle. At 6:00 P.M., the hour and minute hands of a clock are 180° apart. What is the smaller angle between the hour and minute hands of a clock at 6:15 P.M.?

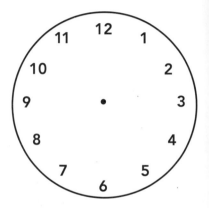

8. Three-syllable rhyme time! If a yearly how-to book is an ANNUAL MANUAL, what is an evil pastor?

9. What completes this pattern?

7 3 8 F 2 Q 3 Q 2 F 8 3 ____

10. What letter should go in the blank?

RAP + PER + EAR = R
CUD + DOC + DUO = D
OAR + RAT + OAT = ____

11. In the grid are hidden 5 five-letter words in a continuous closed path that does not cross itself. Go from letter to letter horizontally, vertically, or diagonally. What are the five words?

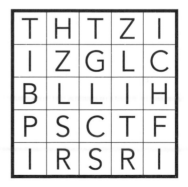

12. What word with two hyphens might be clued punnily as "The sort of fight nobody should pay to see"?

13. Which of A, B, or C comes next in this sequence?

A	B	C

  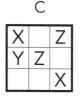

14. Add the same vowel four times to NWRSDT to make the first and last names of a former world leader. Do not rearrange the letters.

15. Anagram the red word in this sentence to make a word that fits in the blank.

The mediums at the seances were beginners, but they'd all read a book titled *Fortune-Telling for* _____.

1. DRAPERY

2. (c) WELL
   All of the words form other words when an
   apostrophe is added. The words are SHE'D, WE'RE,
   I'LL, CAN'T, HE'LL, I'D, and WE'LL.

3. TRIO
   The words are PATRIOT and VITRIOL.

4. GROWER and GROCER

5. I'M AN AC/DC FAN.
   For the first letter of the message, move two
   letters back in the alphabet; for the next letter of
   the message, move two letters forward. Continue
   alternating two back, two forward, and so on.
   (AC/DC is the name of a musical group.)

6. Friday

There are 7 days in a week, so 9 weeks is exactly 63 days. In 63 days, it will be Wednesday again. In 65 days, it will be Friday.

7. 97.5°

At 6:15 P.M., the minute hand points at the 3, and the hour hand is ¼ of the way between the 6 and the 7. There are 360° ÷ 12 = 30° between each pair of adjacent numbers on a clock, and ¼ of 30° is 7.5°. Therefore, the angle between the hands is (3 × 30°) + 7.5° = 97.5°.

8. SINISTER MINISTER

9. 7

The entire sequence is a palindrome (reads the same backward and forward).

10. A

It is the only letter that appears in all three words in the last row. Another way to approach the problem is to cancel out pairs of letters; the answer is the letter left over.

11. ZILCH, FIRST, CRISP, BLITZ, LIGHT

12. FREE-FOR-ALL

13. A

In each successive box, the letters change from W to X to Y to Z and back to W again.

14. ANWAR SADAT
    The letter A is added four times.

15. DUMMIES

1. What are the next two terms in this sequence?

3   11   Q   5   10   R   7   9   S   9   8   T   ___   ___

2. What two different letters can be put in the blank, each forming a four-letter word that can be defined as "pants part"?

S E A ___

3. Which word is the odd one out?

LOSE	CRAP
TUTOR	KEPI
DREAD	AUNT

4. Four regular dice are used to encode the words FOIL, INFO, and LONG. Study the encoding scheme and then decode the last four-letter word.

FOIL

INFO

LONG

_____

GOLF

5. GARNISH becomes TARNISH when you change its first letter from a G to a T. What nine-letter word meaning "begin" becomes a word meaning "end" when you change its first letter from a G to a T?

6. Solv this unusual crossword.

¹	²	³	⁴
⁵			
⁶			
⁷			

ACROSS
1. Scalp tickts
5. Rspctd
6. Tit-for-tat punishmnt
7. Happnings

DOWN
1. St asid
2. Dirctor Spilbrg
3. Priodic tabl itm
4. Projcting shlvs

7. What four-letter country can you put in the blank to form a word meaning "cause to develop"?

IN _____ TE

8. Think of a word that fits in the first blank, and add two letters to the end to form the word for the second blank. What are the two words?

As a chef, I have acquired a certain amount of _____ in using both a wok and a _____.

9. What two-word phrase is represented by these pairs?

DV, OI, US, BI, LO, EN

10. Rearrange these letters to form two words that are antonyms:

THY   VILE   HAG

11. What element of the periodic table does a wordplay expert get by combining the elements iridium, oxygen, and nitrogen?

12. What four-letter word ending in L is related to both film projection and casting?

___ ___ ___ L

13. Suppose you play a 3-D game of tic-tac-toe in a 4-by-4-by-4 cube. How many possible winning lines of four-in-a-row are there?

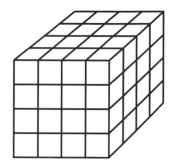

14. Peter, 12 years old, is four times as old as his sister. How old will Peter be when he is twice as old as his sister?

15. What two three-letter words can be inserted into the blanks to form two different seven-letter words?

CA _____ ET   CA _____ ET

ANSWERS 9

1. **11 and 7**
   These are three sequences interspersed:
   3 5 7 9 11, 11 10 9 8 7, and Q R S T.

2. **M, T**
   Both a SEAM and the SEAT are part of a pair of pants.

3. **DREAD**
   The words anagram to give: SOLE, TROUT, ADDER, CARP, PIKE, TUNA. The adder is the only snake among the fish.

4. **KING**
   The sum of the pips showing is the position of the letter in the alphabet. The pips on the first die in the mystery word sum to 6 + 3 + 2 = 11, so the first letter of the word is the 11th letter of the alphabet, K. The remaining calculations are 1 + 5 + 3 = 9 = I; 5 + 3 + 6 = 14 = N; and 4 + 2 + 1 = 7 = G.

5. GERMINATE (becoming TERMINATE)

6. The clues suggest leaving out all of the E's. All of the answers to the clues contain only the vowel E. The words across are RESELL, ESTEEMED, REVENGE, and EVENTS. The words down are RESERVE, STEVEN, ELEMENT, and LEDGES.

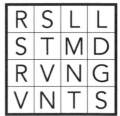

7. CUBA
   The word is INCUBATE.

8. SKILL, SKILLET

9. DOUBLE VISION
   The first letters of the pairs spell DOUBLE. The second letters of the pairs spell VISION.

10. HEAVY, LIGHT

11. IRON
    Their chemical symbols are Ir, O, N.

12. REEL
   A reel holds the film used in film projection. The casting here does not involve filmmaking but casting for fish with a rod and reel.

13. 76 winning lines
   Method 1:
   - 16 straight lines through the cube from each of the top, side, and front faces, making 48 winning lines
   - 2 diagonals on each of the four 4×4 slices in each of the three directions, making 24 more winning lines
   - 4 diagonals of the entire cube, starting at any one of the top corners and proceeding through the cube to the opposite bottom corner
   The total is 48 + 24 + 4 = 76 winning lines.

   Method 2:
   Enclose the 4×4×4 cube in a 6×6×6 shell. Each winning line is surrounded by a pair of cubes opposite each other in the shell, and neither of those cubes is part of any other line. There are 36 + (4 × 20) + 36 = 152 cubes in the shell. Since each pair corresponds to a winning line, there are 152 ÷ 2 = 76 winning lines.

14. 18 years old

Peter is 12 and his sister is 3. Their ages are 9 years apart, and will always be 9 years apart. When Peter is double his sister's age, his sister's age will be the same as the number of years between them. So at that time, Peter will be 18 and his sister will be 9.

15. BAR and BIN, forming CABARET and CABINET

TEST 10

1. Figure out how to create the five answers concealed in these three columns.

Column 1	Column 2	Column 3
TEA	ORB	EAR
PAN	ART	PEN
RAD	RAP	RAP
MOT	CEO	ART
FOR	DAB	OAT

2. Give a common four-letter word made up of four consecutive letters of the alphabet, in some order.

3. Find the two-word lunch dish that is hiding backward in the following sentence:

> The gentleman uttered a terrible comment to Oscar.

4. Which of A, B, or C comes next in this sequence?

A   B   C

5. What are the next two terms in this sequence?

H M I K J I K G L E M C ___ ___

6. Match each picture in the top row with a picture in the bottom row by writing letters in the blanks.

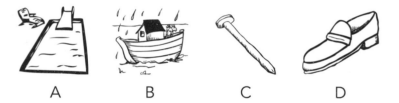

A   B   C   D

7. I have a number of cookies. I eat one, and then give half of the remaining cookies to Sally. Then I eat 2 more, and give half of the remaining cookies to Gary. Now I have 6 cookies left. How many cookies did I begin with?

8. Fill in two different letters to complete two different six-letter words reading clockwise or counterclockwise. What are the words?

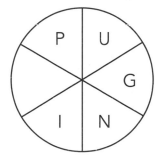

9. Waldo of "Where's Waldo?" fame has a little-known sister named Wanda. You may never have played "Where's Wanda?" For example, she can be found lurking in the phrase BOW AND ARROW. Give another hidden WANDA three-word phrase meaning "occasionally."

10. What three-letter word can follow each of these words to form six new words?

PILL ___ ___ ___   MAN ___ ___ ___

MASS ___ ___ ___   PLUM ___ ___ ___

SEW ___ ___ ___   BAND ___ ___ ___

11. Four views of the same block are shown. Draw the correct front face on the final block.

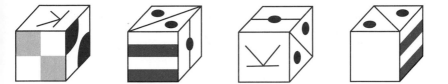

12. If "L B at F" means "Life begins at forty," then what proverb is this?

H W L by the S, D by the S.

13. What famous quotation can be made by rearranging these pictures?

14. Start with the Pakistani city KARACHI. Remove the first and last letters and replace them with two other letters to form a common word. What is the word?

15. The same pair of letters can be inserted side by side into each of these four words, forming a new word each time. What pair of letters is it?

SOLAR

DRAMA

MAINE

CATER

1. Choose one word from each column and combine them to form a word or phrase:
   tear apart (TEA + RAP + ART)
   panda bear (PAN + DAB + EAR)
   radar trap (RAD + ART + RAP)
   motorboat (MOT + ORB + OAT)
   force open (FOR + CEO + PEN)

2. RUST
   The consecutive letters are R, S, T, U.

3. TUNA MELT
   The phrase is hidden backward in
   "genTLEMAN UTtered."

4. B
   The top row and right column stay fixed. The
   positions of the four squares in the bottom left corner
   rotate clockwise.

5. **N and A**
   These are two sequences interspersed:
   H I J K L M N (increasing by 1 at each step) and
   M K I G E C A (decreasing by 2 at each step)

6. **C B D A**
   The words represented by the pictures form pairs of
   rhyming words.
   > POOL & SCHOOL
   > ARK & SHARK
   > NAIL & PAIL
   > SHOE & GLUE

7. **29 cookies**
   Work backward: $6 \times 2 = 12$, then $12 + 2 = 14$, then
   $14 \times 2 = 28$, then $28 + 1 = 29$.

8. **IMPUGN and UPPING**
   For IMPUGN, insert an M and read clockwise
   from the I. For UPPING, insert a P and read
   counterclockwise from the U.

9. **NOW AND AGAIN**

10. AGE

The words formed are PILLAGE, MASSAGE, SEWAGE, MANAGE, PLUMAGE, and BANDAGE.

11.

12. He who lives by the sword, dies by the sword.

13. "To be or not to be," from Hamlet's famous soliloquy in Shakespeare's play, can be formed phonetically from the pictures:

14. EARACHE

15. CH
    The new words are sCHolar, draCHma, maCHine, and catCHer.

TEST 11

1. This is a two-part question. First, find four hidden five-letter words; then figure out what they have in common. To find the four words hidden vertically, take one letter from each of the five words below, in order. You can cross off each letter as you use it, since no letter is used more than once.

```
H E R S
H O O T
H E R O
S E M I
S E C T
```

The four words are _____, _____, _____, and _____. What they have in common is: _____.

2. Which anagram is the odd one out?

GHEU   TELLIT   TAGER

SCOLLOAS   CITAGING   VESMAIS

3. Which of A, B, or C comes next in this sequence?

maraschino, apricot, mayonnaise, juniper, julep, _____

A. sundae
B. augur
C. wedge

4. We've removed all of the vowels from a familiar saying and closed up the spaces. What saying is it?

B S N C M K S T H H R T G R W F N D R

5. Anagram the red word in this sentence to make a word that fits in the blank.

It was irksome to go from an asphyxiating restaurant to a bar that was even _____.

6. HIPS and LIPS are two four-letter body parts that differ only in their first letter. Name two other four-letter body parts that differ only in their first letter.

7. PHEROMONE and HORMONE both end in -MONE. Name another word that ends with the four letters MONE.

8. What is the next term in this sequence?

    2   6   12   20   30   42   56   72   ____

9. Fill in the blanks with six common words by following the pattern set by the first equation.

OVER + THING = THUNDERING

GAIN + COAL = _____

BEGIN + OFFER = _____

FAT + CLOG = _____

HEAVEN + SAC = _____

HIGH + SPOKE = _____

WIMPS + VET = _____

10. Fran has created her own language, in which the order of the words is random. "Callo bymo abba" means "odd new language." "Sintu kipple callo" means "new funny words." "Bymo loovy vauk" means "strange language time." What does "abba" mean?

11. Change one letter in each of these words to make a familiar threesome:

HOT   SKID   RUMP

12. Listen up! After rearranging the letters below, you'll have a seven-letter word meaning "to leave secretly." Hear, hear! What's the word?

OBEDIENCY   ESSAY

13. What pair of letters correctly fills the vacant spot?

ab	ef
gh	mn

di	fu
ou	em

ca	si
li	on

te	ve
sh	

14. Change each three-letter group into a seven-letter word by putting the same pair of letters before and after. Definitions appear, in no particular order, in the second column. If you complete all four words correctly, the pairs of letters, reading down, form an eight-letter bonus word whose definition also appears in the list.

___ Y L I ___	Tooth filler
___ Q U I ___	Gushed
___ A L G ___	Hairdresser
___ I F I ___	Morally uplifted
Bonus word: _____	Need

15. Actress Julia Roberts is harboring a liar (JULIA ROBERTS). What cultural icon who might agree that "Haste makes waste" surprisingly conceals HASTE? (Hint: She's a one-woman industry.)

ANSWERS 11

1. HORSE, ETHIC, ROOMS, SHEET
   HORSE, for example, is found by taking H from HERS,
   O from HOOT, R from HERO, S from SEMI, and E
   from SECT. What the four words have in common
   is WORK. The four words can all be preceded by
   the word WORK to make new words or phrases:
   workhorse, work ethic, workrooms, work sheet.

2. TELLIT
   The letter groups can be rearranged to spell HUGE,
   LITTLE, GREAT, COLOSSAL, GIGANTIC, and
   MASSIVE. All of them mean "big," except for LITTLE.

3. B. augur
   The words in the sequence begin with three-letter
   month abbreviations: MARaschino, APRicot,
   MAYonnaise, JUNiper, JULep, AUGur.

4. Absence makes the heart grow fonder.

5. SMOKIER

6. CHIN and SHIN

7. ANEMONE

8. 90

Method 1
The sequence is 1×2, 2×3, 3×4, 4×5, 5×6, 6×7, 7×8, 8×9. The calculation for the answer is 9 × 10 = 90.

Method 2
Keep adding the next even number in the sequence 4, 6, 8, 10, 12, 14, 16. The calculation for the answer is 72 + 18 = 90.

9. The words are COLOSSAL, OFFENDER, CLOTHING, SHELLAC, SLOWPOKE, and VEHEMENT. In each case, put the antonym of the first word somewhere inside the second word.
GAIN + COAL = CO(LOSS)AL
BEGIN + OFFER = OFF(END)ER
FAT + CLOG = CLO(THIN)G
HEAVEN + SAC = S(HELL)AC
HIGH + SPOKE = S(LOW)POKE
WIMPS + VET = VE(HE-MEN)T

10. "*Abba*" means "odd."

> *Callo bymo abba* = odd new language
> *Bymo loovy vauk* = strange language time

"*Bymo*," the only word appearing in both the first and third statements, must mean "language."

> *Callo bymo abba* = odd new language
> *Sintu kipple callo* = new funny words

"*Callo*," the only word appearing in both the first and second statements, must mean "new."

> *Callo bymo abba* = odd new language

The only word remaining in the first statement is "*abba*," so it must mean "odd."

11. HOP, SKIP, JUMP

12. ABSCOND
    As the question suggests, you need to "hear" the seven letters. If you say "obediency essay" out loud, it sounds like O B D N C S A. These seven letters can be rearranged to form the answer, ABSCOND.

13. ic

Words are formed by reading across the boxes located in the same position in each square. Reading the upper left boxes in order spells ABDICATE. Reading the upper right boxes in order spells EFFUSIVE. Reading the lower left boxes in order spells GHOULISH. Reading the lower right corner boxes in order spells MNEMON___. The only letter pair that can fill the blank to form a word is "ic," spelling MNEMONIC.

14. STYLIST (hairdresser)
REQUIRE (need)
AMALGAM (tooth filler)
EDIFIED (morally uplifted)
Bonus word: STREAMED (gushed)

15. MARTHA STEWART

TEST 12

1. What anagram of FEEL VERY LOW is a two-word disease that might make you feel very low?

2. Think of a word that fits in the first blank, and remove two letters from the end to form the word for the second blank. What are the two words?

   The reporter came on TV with a news
   _____ saying that the police retrieved
   the _____, but not the gun.

3. What two-word phrase meaning "little kids" becomes a fast food order when the second word is pluralized?

4. We found a bunch of "head" words, but the artist drew the pictures in the wrong places. Can you figure out what the words are supposed to be?

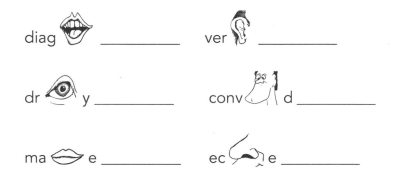

diag _____   ver _____

dr y _____   conv d _____

ma e _____   ec e _____

5. The word DECIDE in block capitals has horizontal symmetry. What six-letter word for something really cool, but no longer in use, also exhibits horizontal symmetry when written in block capitals?

6. Which of A, B, or C comes next in this sequence?

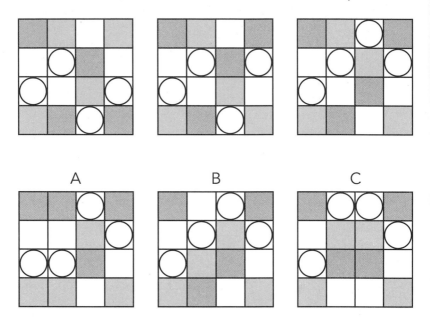

A   B   C

7. Here's a no-brainer. Take the words NO BRAINER, ignore the space, change two letters, and respace the result to make a famous director. Who is it?

8. In the diagram below, ball A moves clockwise, one position at a time. If ball A lands on a shaded area, ball B moves two places clockwise. If ball A lands on an unshaded area, ball B moves three places counterclockwise. If ball B lands on a shaded area, ball C moves three places clockwise. If ball B lands on an unshaded area, ball C moves two places counterclockwise. Over the next six moves of ball A, what six-letter word is spelled out by ball C?

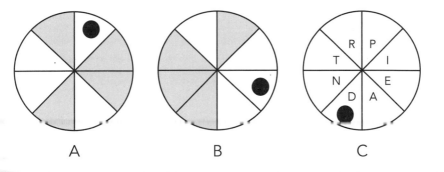

A   B   C

9. In the grid are hidden 5 five-letter words in a continuous closed path that does not cross itself. Go from letter to letter horizontally, vertically, or diagonally. What are the five words?

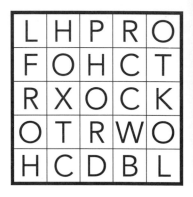

L	H	P	R	O
F	O	H	C	T
R	X	O	C	K
O	T	R	W	O
H	C	D	B	L

10. In line for a movie, I am 12th from the front and 18th from the end. How many people are in line?

11. What common two-word warning could you give to people who are too introspective?

12. What is the next term in this sequence?

243 162 108 72 48 ____

13. Fill in the missing letters to form two world countries:

_____NADA   _____NADA

14. Joe and Paula wed, and both had children from previous marriages. After some years, the family increased to 10 children. At this point, Joe had 7 children of his own and Paula had 6 children of her own. How many children were born since Joe and Paula's marriage?

15.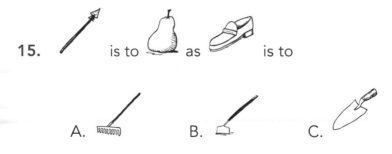

A.   B.   C.

1. YELLOW FEVER

2. BULLETIN, BULLET

3. Small fry (which becomes "small fries")

4. diagNOSE, drEARy, maCHINe, verMOUTH, convEYEd, ecLIPSe

   The incorrect versions given were diag(MOUTH), dr(EYE)y, ma(LIPS)e, ver(EAR), conv(CHIN)d, and ec(NOSE)e.

5. ICEBOX

6. A

   From the first pattern to the next, the only difference is that the right-hand column is inverted. In the next pattern, the column second from the right is inverted. To continue the pattern, we invert the column second from the left.

7. ROB REINER

Change the first N in NO BRAINER to an R, and the A to an E, then respace.

8. REPAIR

Interestingly, although the wheels for A and B are different, their pattern of shaded and unshaded landings is the same while spelling out the word. If S = shaded and U = unshaded, the landings are:

A	B	C
S	S	R
S	S	E
U	U	P
S	S	A
U	U	I
U	U	R

9. TORCH, PHLOX, FROTH, CROWD, BLOCK

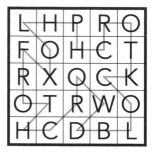

10. 29

There are 11 before me and 17 behind me. The total is 11 + 1 + 17 = 29.

11. Look out!

12. 32

Every term is ⅔ of the term before it.

13. CANADA and GRENADA

14. 3

The calculation is $(7 + 6) - 10 = 3$. Here's why. The sum $(7 + 6)$ represents all of Joe and Paula's children by previous marriages, plus twice the number of children they had with each other (the overlapping children are counted twice when you add $7 + 6$). If we subtract 10 from this sum, we eliminate each child once. The remaining amount, one "overlap," is the number of children Joe and Paula had together.

15. B

Remove the initial S in each case: SPEAR is to PEAR as SHOE is to HOE.

TEST 13

1. Give an appropriate order for these three-letter chunks:

   INS   ING   LEF   ILE

2. Fill in a letter to complete a common word reading clockwise or counterclockwise. What is the word?

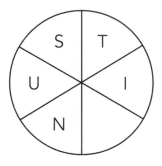

3. What is the next term in this sequence?

$$2 \quad 3 \quad 5 \quad 9 \quad 17 \quad 33 \quad 65 \quad \underline{\quad}$$

4. Room A contains 7 people. Room B contains the number of people in A plus half the number of people in C. Room C contains the same number of people as Room A and Room B combined. How many people combined are there in Rooms A, B, and C?

5. Two of these proverbs have nearly opposite meanings. Which two?

    A. Every cloud has a silver lining.
    B. Clothes make the man.
    C. Where there's smoke, there's fire.
    D. Don't judge a book by its cover.
    E. Actions speak louder than words.

6. Match each picture in the top row with a word in the bottom row by writing letters in the blanks.

A   B   C   D

___   ___   ___   ___

phoniness nanosecond automaton permanent

7. What mysterious seven-letter word is represented here?

$$-5 \quad +2 \quad +9 \quad P \quad +4 \quad -1 \quad -2$$

8. Take the letters of the word INSET twice. Rearrange all 10 letters to form a part of the body.

9. Solve ths unusual crossword.

1	2	3	4
5			
6			
7			

ACROSS
1. Has dffculty sayng "S"
5. Desre
6. Pece of cake
7. Lke an uncomfortable collar

DOWN
1. Prohbted
2. Downhll or cross-country actvty
3. Small recpe amount
4. Vson

10. A five-letter word meaning "joins together" is made of a two-letter approval inside a three-letter approval. What is the five-letter word?

11. What one-word anagram of IN RANGE means "moving in range"?

12. A 61 × 69-cm painting is made up of nine squares, as shown. The upper left square is 28 × 28 cm. Find the dimensions of the other eight squares.

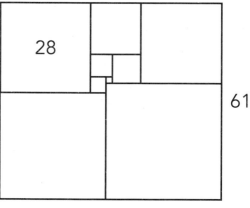

13. You can interweave the words MEAN and CHIC to form MECHANIC. Both words remain in left-to-right order in the longer word. What two four-letter words were interwoven to form FRIENDLY?

14. The numbers in the diagrams combine in the same way to make correct arithmetic statements. What number is missing from the last diagram?

15. Add one straight line below to make the name of a city.

1. IN SINGLE FILE
   Just respace the chunks without rearranging them.

2. SUNLIT
   Insert an L and read counterclockwise from S.

3. 129
   Method 1: These are powers of 2, increased by 1. The next term is $2^7 + 1 = 129$.

   Method 2: Keep adding the next power of 2. The next term is $65 + 64 = 129$.

   Method 3: Multiply each successive number by 2 and subtract 1. The next term is $(65 \times 2) - 1 = 129$.

4. 56
   If X equals half the people in room C, then A has 7 people, B has 7 + X people, and C has X + X people. According to the third sentence, C has 14 + X. Comparing the C's, X = 14. The total is 7 + 21 + 28 = 56 people.

5. B and D

6. BDAC

The words represented by the pictures are hidden inside the words given. That is, NOSE is inside naNOSEcond, NINE in phoNINEss, MANE in perMANEnt, and TOMATO in auTOMATOn.

7. KRYPTON

The central P is the reference point. K is 5 before P, so –5 represents K. R is 2 after P, so +2 represents R, and so on.

8. INTESTINES

9. The clues suggest leaving out all of the I's. All of the answers to the clues contain only the vowel I. The words across are LISPS, LIKING, CINCH, and TIGHT. The words down are ILLICIT, SKIING, PINCH, and SIGHT.

10. YOKES

The word is made up of OK inside YES.

11. NEARING

12.

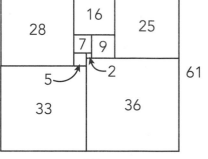

Since the left edge totals 61 cm, and the top left square has edge 28, we know that the bottom left square has edge 61 − 28 = 33. Along the bottom, the total is 69 cm, so the bottom right square has edge length 69 − 33 = 36. Continuing to spiral in, the top right square has edge 61 − 36 = 25, the middle top square has edge 61 − (28 + 25) = 16. Use common edges of squares known to finish the calculations. We have 25 − 16 = 9, then 16 − 9 = 7, then 9 − 7 = 2, and finally 7 − 2 = 5.

13. FIND and RELY

14. 2

Add the shaded number and the circled number. In each case, this sum is the same as the product of the numbers in the two unshaded squares. The calculation for the missing number is $(6 \times 1) - 4 = 2$.

15.

Add the line down the middle and look at the entire thing upside down to find the answer, RIO.

TEST 14

1. Each word clued below consists of five letters, with middle letter A. Each word's last two letters overlap with the first two letters of another word. We've given the clues in random order. Fit the words in overlapping form around the circle clockwise, one letter per blank. We've already inserted the A's for you.

- Arrive at
- Stock market unit
- Hide away for safekeeping
- Huge meal
- Make sore by rubbing

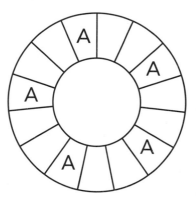

2. Make 5 seven-letter words by inserting each three-letter word in the top row into the exact center of one of the four-letter words in the bottom row. (For example, NOT inside DEED makes DENOTED.)

BOO   IRE   ONE   RED   YEN
BOOM   CANE   CASE   FAST   PIER

3. What seven-letter kitchen appliance becomes less interesting when you change its third letter from an E to an A?

4. Which anagram is the odd one out?

ADS   MULG   MISLAD   SOOMER   REFLEUCH

5. What is the next term in this sequence?

II   IV   VI   VIII   X   XII   XIV   ___

6. In the grid are hidden 5 five-letter words in a continuous closed path that does not cross itself. Go from letter to letter horizontally, vertically, or diagonally. What are the five words?

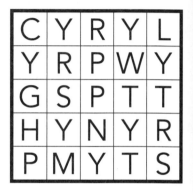

7. You might wish you had a calculator for this! If SIZZLE is worth 372215, then what country is worth 321738?

8. What common phrase is represented by the circled letters in the five oceans here?

PAⒸIFIⒸ
ATLANTIⒸ
INDIAN
ARⒸTIⒸ
ANTARⒸTIⒸ

9. What two different letters can each be put in the blank to form a six-letter word that can be defined as "fire starter"?

＿＿＿ I N D E R

10. The numbers in the diagrams combine in the same way to make correct arithmetic statements. What number is missing from the last diagram?

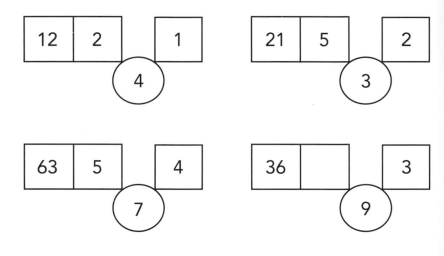

| 12 | 2 | | 1 |
| 4 |

| 21 | 5 | | 2 |
| 3 |

| 63 | 5 | | 4 |
| 7 |

| 36 | | | 3 |
| 9 |

11. Which of A, B, or C comes next in this sequence?

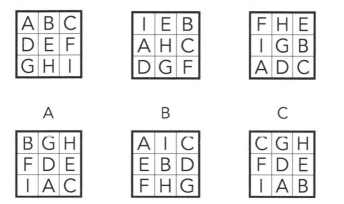

12. Anagram the red word in this sentence to make a word that fits in the blank.

I'm going to _____ to the gym manager that the spotter isn't always watching me when I'm on the trampoline.

13. The large rectangle is divided into four smaller rectangles. The numbers represent the areas of the smaller rectangles. What is the area of the lower left rectangle? (Note: The diagram is not to scale.)

12	27
	63

14. BONGO HAD HI CODED IHHQ NCDUE NEA'C PDQ?

1. PRQNEO

2. XNADRXXZD

3. GODPPS

4. KDDC

5. CHURCH

6. ECPRBKDPPS

15. Remove a two-letter chunk from the interior of each of these eight-letter words, always leaving a six-letter word. Cross off the removed letters from the alphabet given. When you're finished, four letters will remain. They can be rearranged to spell a bonus word having to do with pairs. What is the bonus word?

A B C D E F G H I J K L M N O P Q R S T U V W X Y Z

ADMIRING	EXPLICIT	FORCIBLE
GROWNUPS	HIJACKER	PIGSTIES
VANQUISH	RELEVANT	SELFSAME
	SKYLIGHT	SNEEZERS

ANSWERS 14

1. The words are REACH, SHARE, STASH, FEAST, and CHAFE. (Your filled diagram may be a rotation of ours.)

2. BOREDOM, CAYENNE, CABOOSE, FAIREST, PIONEER

3. BLENDER
   Changing the E in the third spot to A makes the blender BLANDER.

4. REFLEUCH
   The letter groups can be arranged to spell SAD, GLUM, DISMAL, MOROSE, and CHEERFUL. These all mean "unhappy" except CHEERFUL.

5. XVI

   The series consists of the even numbers, written in Roman numerals.

6. CRYPT, WRYLY, TRYST, NYMPH, GYPSY

7. BELIZE

   Type each number into a calculator and turn the calculator upside down to see the words.

8. The Seven Seas (C's)

9. C and T

   Both a CINDER and TINDER could start a fire.

10. 1

Divide the left-hand boxed number by the circled number, and subtract the right-hand boxed number. The calculation for the final answer is $(36 \div 9) - 3 = 1$.

11. C

The pattern snakes in an S shape through the grid, moving down the left column, up the middle column, and back down the right column. Letters disappearing at the bottom right reappear again at the top left.

12. PROTEST

13. 28

Look for common factors in the given numbers to find the lengths of the sides of the rectangles. The only common factor of 12 and 27 is 3, so the two upper rectangles measure 3×4 and 3×9, which means the lower right rectangle measures 7×9. The area of the fourth rectangle, therefore, is $4 \times 7 = 28$.

14. 2 or PINEAPPLE

This is a simple substitution code. The first word is likely to be a question word; a question word with the same substitution pattern as BONGO is WHICH. Look for common letter patterns to crack the rest of the code. The translated question is "WHICH ONE OF THESE FOOD ITEMS ISN'T RED? 1. RADISH 2. PINEAPPLE 3. CHERRY 4. BEET 5. TOMATO 6. STRAWBERRY"

15. BOTH

DM taken from ADMIRING makes AIRING.
XP taken from EXPLICIT makes ELICIT.
RC taken from FORCIBLE makes FOIBLE.
WN taken from GROWNUPS makes GROUPS.
IJ taken from HIJACKER makes HACKER.
GS taken from PIGSTIES makes PITIES.
QU taken from VANQUISH makes VANISH.
VA taken from RELEVANT makes RELENT.
LF taken from SELFSAME makes SESAME.
KY taken from SKYLIGHT makes SLIGHT.
ZE taken from SNEEZERS makes SNEERS.
The unused letters are B, H, O, and T, which can be anagrammed to spell only one word, BOTH.

TEST 15

1. A sign painter wants to center the word CASHIERS on a 100-cm sign. Each letter is to be 10 cm wide, and there is to be a space of 2 cm between consecutive letters. How many centimeters of space will be left at each end of the sign?

2. Fill in each set of blanks with a different word. The five words added have something in common.

MEAD _ _ _ ARK
MI _ _ _ _ AVE
H _ _ _ _ CUS
INT _ _ _ _ _ OUS
CHRYSANTH _ _ _ M

3. The wordplay fans below are at a dance studio, and each person chooses an appropriate dance partner of the opposite sex. Since there are more men than women, which man doesn't get a partner?

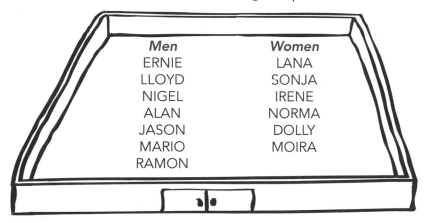

Men	Women
ERNIE	LANA
LLOYD	SONJA
NIGEL	IRENE
ALAN	NORMA
JASON	DOLLY
MARIO	MOIRA
RAMON	

4. What do violins, noses, crossable rivers, and people with dental work have in common?

5. The year 1472, written FOURTEEN SEVENTY-TWO, contains some letters with curves and some without. What is the most recent year that can be similarly written out in words in block capitals, but using no curved letters?

6. Put the same six-letter word in all three lines to form expressions with the word preceding and the word following (such as BEAR SKIN TIGHT). The same word must be used for all three lines.

AIR __ __ __ __ __ __ BOOK

PICK __ __ __ __ __ __ MONEY

HIP __ __ __ __ __ __ PROTECTOR

7. What is the minimum number of identical square tiles needed to tile a rectangular floor measuring 24 × 30?

8. What four-letter word can fill all four blanks to form new words?

_____RUNG   _____ART
_____ORATION   _____RAIN

9. This question has two answers. Insert a six-letter food item, one letter per square, across the middle row of this grid so that six common three-letter words are formed reading down. Then insert a six-letter bird so that, once again, common words are formed reading down. (Hint: Finding one answer will lead you quickly to the other answer.)

A	S	I	A	N	S
T	W	E	E	D	Y

10. Fill in two different letters to complete two different six-letter words, one reading clockwise and one reading counterclockwise. What are the two words?

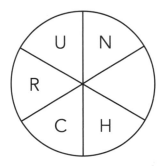

11. What is the final letter in this sequence? (Hint: The entire sequence has only these 12 letters.)

I E L Z L I I Z R N M ____

12. Think of a word that fits in the first blank, and remove two letters from the front to form the word for the second blank. What are the two words?

The _____ looks _____ than those comparatively friendly people from the east.

13. Name a famous Christian whose last name means "someone who does a roofing chore."

14. Name the utensil represented by these letters:

u o o d s

15. Match each picture in the top row with a picture in the bottom row by writing letters in the blanks.

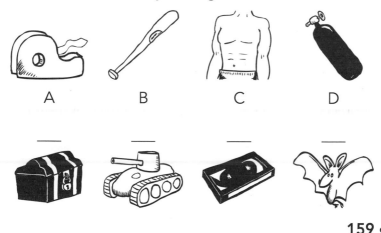

A   B   C   D

ANSWERS 15

1. 3 cm

    The letters use 80 cm. The spaces between letters use 7 × 2 = 14 cm. This is 94 of the 100 cm, leaving 6 cm extra. If the word is centered, then 6 cm of extra space means 3 cm extra at each end.

2. Add five birds—OWL, CROW, IBIS, RAVEN, and EMU— to form MEADOWLARK, MICROWAVE, HIBISCUS, INTRAVENOUS, and CHRYSANTHEMUM.

3. NIGEL

    Since they're wordplay fans, each person dances with someone whose name is an anagram of his or her own: ALAN and LANA, ERNIE and IRENE, JASON and SONJA, LLOYD and DOLLY, MARIO and MOIRA, and RAMON and NORMA, leaving NIGEL unmatched.

4. They all have BRIDGES.

5. 1999 (NINETEEN NINETY-NINE)

6. POCKET

The expressions formed are AIR POCKET, PICKPOCKET, HIP POCKET, POCKETBOOK, POCKET MONEY, and POCKET PROTECTOR.

7. 20

The largest whole number that divides into both 24 and 30 is 6, so you can use square tiles measuring 6 × 6. There will be 4 tiles spanning the width and 5 spanning the length, making 20 tiles in all.

8. REST

The words formed are RESTRUNG, RESTORATION, RESTART, and RESTRAIN.

9. CARROT and PARROT

The words formed reading down are ACT/APT, SAW, IRE, ARE, NOD, and STY. One way to solve this is to list the possibilities for each spot vertically and search for answers reading across. Here's the list of possibilities:

```
C A C C O A
F E R D   H
N O   G   K
P     L   L
R     P   O
      R   P
      T   T
      V
      W
      X
      Y
```

10. CRUNCH and URCHIN

Fill in a C and read clockwise from the other C to spell CRUNCH. Fill in an I and read counterclockwise from the U to spell URCHIN.

11. C

These are the initial letters of the months (J F M A M J J A S O N D) moved back one in the alphabet. The initial letter of December is D. Moving D one letter back gives the answer, C.

12. WESTERNER, STERNER

13. Christian SLATER is an actor who really has a "Christian" name.

14. spoon

Turn the original letters upside-down to see the word.

15. CDAB

The pairs are words with different meanings. Match the Scotch TAPE and cassette TAPE, baseball BAT and flying BAT, human CHEST and treasure CHEST, and the military TANK and gas TANK.

TEST 16

1. What is the next date in this sequence?

   January 4, February 4, March 1, April 2, May 1, June 1, July 2, August 2, _____

2. Will has $20 more than Sue, who has $5 more than Jean. Together, these three people have $90. How much money does Jean have?

3. What four-letter word finishes this analogy?

   ASTOUND is to STUN as UNSIGHTLY is to

   _____.

4. What three-letter word can fill all four blanks to form new words?

ENT_____   D_____ER

SE_____H   _____IER

5. Which is the odd one out?

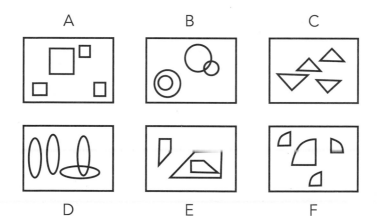

6. The title of a Puccini opera appears as the first five letters of a famous conductor's name. Who's the conductor?

7. What is the only number with its letters in alphabetical order when written out in English?

A B C D E F G H I J K L M N O P Q R S T U V W X Y Z

8. Two numbers have been inserted in the strip of boxes below. I plan to put numbers in the ten remaining boxes so that the numbers in every set of three consecutive boxes total 14. What number goes in the box marked X?

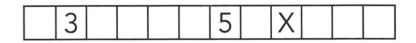

	3					5	X			

9. A square is divided into two squares and two rectangles. The areas of the squares are shown. What is the total area of the two rectangles?

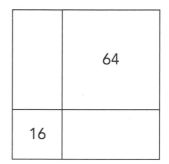

10. What word for a member of a religious order sounds like a type of chicken?

11. At the mixed-up farm:

   The rat made pictures for a gallery.
   The lamb needed some lip ointment.
   The hogs said, "Gee!"
   The horse was at the edge of the water.
   The ewe was tiny.
   What animal wore a Roman garment?

12. What is the next term in this sequence? (Hint: You may have seen this sequence somewhere before.)

A S D F G H J K ____

13. Insert the five vowels A, E, I, O, and U, once each in some order, into each of these three sets of letters to form three new words. You do not need to rearrange the letters. For example, CLFLWR becomes CAULIFLOWER.

PNDMNM _____

LTRVLT _____

TPTNTS _____

14. Anagram the red word in this sentence to make a word that fits in the blank.

Only the most _____ person would add more tarragon without asking the chef first.

15. What five-letter word can be inserted into each set of letters to make three new words?

SMIENS   EAL   FAD

ANSWERS 16

1. September 3
   Each month is followed by its number of syllables.

2. $20
   Will has $25 more than Jean. Sue has $5 more than
   Jean. Together they have $30 more than Jean. If we
   remove their extra $30 from the total $90, then each
   of the three people would have the same amount.
   Jean has $60 ÷ 3 = $20.

3. UGLY
   STUN is a synonym of "astound" found hidden
   left-to-right in ASTOUND (in nonconsecutive letters),
   and UGLY is a synonym of "unsightly" similarly found
   left-to-right in UNSIGHTLY.

4. RAP
   The words formed are ENTRAP, SERAPH, DRAPER,
   and RAPIER.

5. E

It only contains three figures. The rest have four.

6. Arturo TOSCANINI has the opera *Tosca* spelled out at the beginning of his surname.

7. FORTY

8. 6

The calculation is simply $14 - 3 - 5 = 6$. If you fill in a strip of numbers with the stipulation that any three consecutive boxes must total a fixed amount, the numbers must cycle in groups of three, like this:

| A | B | C | A | B | C | A | B | C | A | B | C |

Here's why. If the sum of the first set of three numbers ($A + B + C$) is fixed and equals the sum of the second set of three numbers ($B + C + \star$), then the fourth number ($\star$) must be a repeat of the first number (A), and so forth.

9. 64

A square with area 64 is 8 × 8, and a square with area 16 is 4 × 4. The two rectangles are 4 × 8, so their total area is 64.

10. FRIAR (which sounds like FRYER)

11. GOAT

Each animal anagrams to a word hinted at in the rest of its sentence:

RAT & ART
LAMB & BALM
HOGS & GOSH
HORSE & SHORE
EWE & WEE

A Roman garment is a TOGA, which is an anagram of GOAT.

12. L

You've seen this sequence on the middle row of a typewriter or computer keyboard.

13. PANDEMONIUM, ULTRAVIOLET, OUTPATIENTS

14. ARROGANT

15. THERE
   The words formed are SMITHEREENS, ETHEREAL, and FATHERED.

TEST 17

1. What type of American could be represented by TOMORROW in a cryptogram?

2. What one-word anagram of REDUCTIONS is someone who makes reductions?

3. These four words are encoded in similar but slightly different ways. What are the four words?

NMD

RUM

QEOBB

BKQN

4. Rearrange these letters to form two words that are antonyms.

GLIB TITLE

5. What is the next domino in this sequence?

20	17	14	11	8	5	?
400	289	196	121	64	25	?

6. How should the final cube be marked in this sequence?

7. Make 4 ten-letter words by combining these five-letter words in pairs. For example, TAPES + TRIES = TAPESTRIES.

   AGNES   ASSES   CHAMP   CHART
   LISTS   PASTE   REUSE   SABLE

8. I plan to fill in this strip of boxes with one number per box so that each box (after the first two) is the sum of the two previous boxes. Two numbers have already been inserted. What number goes in the box marked A?

A			18			76	

9. Add two letters in different spots to the word UNIFORM to make a kind of writing.

10. This question has two parts. Find four surnames hidden vertically, then figure out what they have in common. To find the four names, take one letter from each of the five words below, in order. You can cross off each letter as you use it, since no letter is used more than once.

```
G I L A
R E A L
B O I L
G L E N
H E N S
```

The surnames are: _____

What they have in common is: _____

11. What well-known play do you hear when you read these words quickly?

LAME   HISSER   APPLE

12. What numbers go in the empty spaces?

15	13	11	9	7	5	
15	26	33	36	35	30	

13. Change the central letter in each of these six words to make a new word. The new letters spell a common word. What is this six-letter word?

INHABIT
EARNING
SOLVING
WITLESS
TRACTOR
CONVERT

14. A group of office workers split equally the cost of a $72 gift. Later, three more people agreed to contribute, and so the original contributors each got $2 back. How many people were in the original group?

15. Slve this unusual crsswrd.

1	2	3	4
5			
6			
7			

ACRSS
1. Really bad mvies
5. Dwarf frm flklre
6. Drum f Native American rigin: Hyph.
7. Seasnal wind

DWN
1. Fundatin
2. Jseph Smith fllwer
3. Sturdy dr fasteners
4. Wise fellw in the Bible

1. HAWAIIAN

2. DISCOUNTER

3. ONE, TWO, THREE, FOUR
   Move the letters in NMD one forward in the alphabet, the letters in RUM two forward, the letters in QEOBB three forward, and the letters in BKQN four forward.

4. BIG, LITTLE

5.

The top numbers decrease by threes, so the next is 5 – 3 = 2. The bottom number is the square of the top number, so the next is $2^2 = 4$.

6.

The letters on the left face increase by steps of five: D, I, N, S, X. The top letter is two forward from the left-hand letter, and the right-hand letter is three back from the left-hand letter.

7. ASSESSABLE, CHAMPAGNES, CHARTREUSE, PASTELISTS

8. 4

To solve, suppose that X and Y are the numbers between 18 and 76. Then $Y - X = 18$ and $X + Y = 76$. Adding these equations together, we find that $2Y = 94$, so $Y = 47$. Now, work backward. $76 - 47 = 29$; $29 - 18 = 11$; $18 - 11 = 7$; and $11 - 7 = 4$. The completed strip is:

4	7	11	18	29	47	76	123

9. CUNEIFORM
   Cuneiform is the wedge-shaped writing of the ancient Babylonians.

10. The surnames are GABLE, IRONS, LEIGH, and ALLEN. These are all surnames of movie stars (Clark Gable, Jeremy Irons, Vivien Leigh, and Woody Allen).

11. *Les Misérables*

12. 3 and 21
    The numbers in the top row sequentially decrease by two. The numbers in the bottom row are the numbers in the top row multiplied by 1, 2, 3, 4, 5, and 6, respectively. So the next square in the top row is $5 - 2 = 3$ and the next square in the bottom row is $3 \times 7 = 21$.

13. IRONIC
    The new words are INHIBIT, EARRING, SOLOING, WITNESS, TRAITOR, and CONCERT.

14. 9

You could solve this using algebra, but a little trial and error is probably faster. You need two pairs of numbers with a product of 72, where the numbers in the pairs are different by 3 and 2, respectively. The pairs are (9, 8) and (12, 6). Note that 9 and 12 are 3 apart, and 8 and 6 are 2 apart. There were originally 9 people at $8 each, and it turned into 12 people at $6 each.

15. The clues suggest leaving out all of the O's. All of the answers to the clues contain only the vowel O. The words across are BOMBS, TROLL, TOM-TOM, and MONSOON. The words down are BOTTOM, MORMON, BOLTS, and SOLOMON.

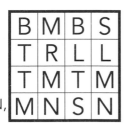

TEST 18

1. What four-letter word can be inserted into each set of letters to make three new words?

SESS   FLCO   FILT

2. What four-letter word finishes this analogy?

ANTS is to BOUT as INKS is to _____.

3. What triplet finishes this sequence?

LET, IGO, LUE, EEN, LOW, NGE, _____

4. To spell a nine-letter word in each grid below, spiral clockwise around the perimeter, adding letters in the empty boxes, and finish in the central square. Each word begins on a letter given in one of the four corners. (You must decide which corner to begin with, but always start on a letter, not at an empty box.) The four answer words are all related.

5. You're one of 17 people, each of whom is told to stand on a number in the circle shown. One of you will receive a gift by an elimination method, which you've secretly learned. The person on spot 1 is eliminated, and then every third person (4, 7, etc.) is eliminated until only one person remains. Which circle should you stand on to be sure of winning the gift?

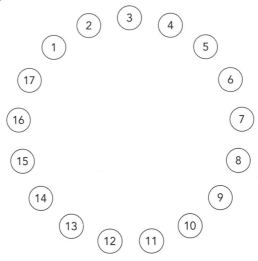

6. Which anagram is the odd one out?

LECKIN   PYNNE   PAMST   TRARQUE   MEDI

7. Insert a seven-letter animal, one letter per square, across the top row of this grid so that seven common three-letter words are formed reading down.

A	N	E	R	O	I	D
B	E	D	E	W	E	D

8. What are the next two terms in this sequence?

11   6   12   7   14   9   18   13   26   ____   ____

9. By inserting three addition signs into the numbers 1 2 3 4 5 6, you can make a sum of 75 like this: 12 + 3 + 4 + 56. Find a different way to insert three addition signs to form a sum of 75.

1   2   3   4   5   6

10. Rearrange TENDER NAME to form a word meaning "tender name."

11. Two of these proverbs have nearly opposite meaning. Which two?

    A. East, west, home's best.
    B. Absence makes the heart grow fonder.
    C. Truth is stranger than fiction.
    D. Cold hands, warm heart.
    E. Out of sight, out of mind.

12. If this figure were to be cut out and folded along the lines to form a cube, what would be the letter on the face opposite the face labeled A?

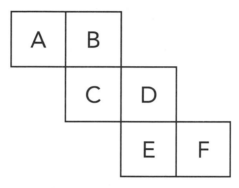

13. Find two different parts of a kitchen sink that fit this pattern.

___ ___ ___ I N

14. Each number in this sequence refers to the makeup of the number above it. What is the next term in the sequence?

1
11
21
1112
3112
211213
312213
212223
114213
31121314

_____

15. If you rotate the first figure 90° clockwise and hold it in front of a mirror, which of A, B, C, or D is the image you will see in the mirror?

A

B

C

D

1. AMEN
   The words formed are SAMENESS, FLAMENCO, and FILAMENT.

2. JOLT
   Move each letter one forward in the alphabet. ANTS changes to BOUT by shifting each letter one forward. Similarly, INKS changes to JOLT.

3. RED
   These are the last three letters of each of the colors in the visible spectrum, listed in reverse order (vioLET, indIGO, bLUE, grEEN, yelLOW, oraNGE, RED).

4. SINGAPORE, ARGENTINA, SWAZILAND, VENEZUELA
   These are all countries.

5. 9

The order of elimination is: 1, 4, 7, 10, 13, 16, 3, 8, 12, 17, 6, 14, 5, 15, 11, 2.

6. PAMST

The letter groups can be arranged to spell NICKEL, PENNY, STAMP, QUARTER, and DIME. These are all coins, except the stamp.

7. GORILLA

The words formed are GAB, ONE, RED, IRE, LOW, LIE, ADD. There are too many letter possibilities to list here, but the best approach to solving this is to note that only O can precede NE to make a word, and that the last letter must be A or O, which narrows down the number of animal possibilities considerably.

8. 21 and 42

The pattern is to subtract 5, multiply by 2, subtract 5, multiply by 2, and so on.

9. 1 + 23 + 45 + 6

10. ENDEARMENT

11. B and E

12. D

13. BASIN and DRAIN
Both are five-letter words ending in IN that are parts of a kitchen sink.

14. 41122314
Each number describes the numbers comprising the number above it. For instance, 3112 is directly above 211213. 3112 is made up of two 1's, one 2, and one 3. If we write that out using digits (2 1's, 1 2, and 1 3), and then simplify the notation by dropping everything *but* the digits, we get 21 12 13. Delete the spaces and you have the next number in the series, 211213. Then, since 211213 is made of three 1's, two 2's and one 3 (3 1's, 2 2's, and 1 3), the next term of the sequence is 312213. The last term given is 31121314, which has 4 1's, 1 2, 2 3's, and 1 4, so the next term is 41122314.

15. B

Try it yourself with a mirror!

TEST 19

1. $(G + \sqrt{Y}) \div D$ equals what?

      1. A   2. B   3. C   4. D   5. E

2. A mug filled with substance X weighs 500 grams. The same mug filled with substance Y weighs 350 grams. If substance X is twice as heavy as substance Y, how much does the empty mug weigh?

3. What major Canadian city's name can be made from only the letters in the second half of the alphabet?

    N O P Q R S T U V W X Y Z

4. Change one letter in each of these words to make a familiar threesome.

SMELL   TEDIUM   BARGE

5. Fill in two different letters to complete two different six-letter words, one reading clockwise and one reading counterclockwise. What are the two words?

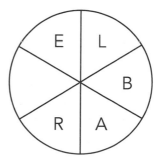

6. What six-letter sport becomes a sport participant when you shift its first letter two letters forward in the alphabet?

7. What triplet finishes this unusual sequence?

   HAT, LET, HES, HIS, UAL, _____

8. What number completes the final column of this diagram?

19	I	1	E	21	S	4	M
F	16	X	20	D	6	U	

9. You'll love the answer to this one!

8215   25725   623462

10. I plan to visit six friends—A, B, C, D, E, and F—each friend visited once.

- I visit B before I visit A, and I visit A before I visit D.
- I visit C after I visit E.
- I visit F fourth.
- I don't visit D last.
- I visit A immediately before I visit E.

In what order do I visit my six friends?

11. Think of a word that fits in the first blank, and add one letter to the end to form the word for the second blank. What are the two words?

The synagogue's _____ owned a pet _____.

12. Which of A, B, C, or D has the unusual property shared by the six words in the first column?

PAST   A. HIND
WHO   B. PARK
TEMPER   C. SWAM
ARE   D. TRIP
CHIN
DRAM

13. Match each picture in the top row with a word in the bottom row by writing letters in the blanks.

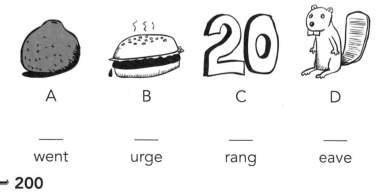

A	B	C	D
___	___	___	___
went	urge	rang	eave

14. 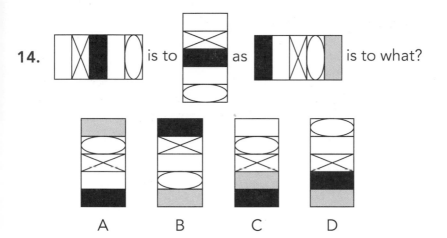 is to 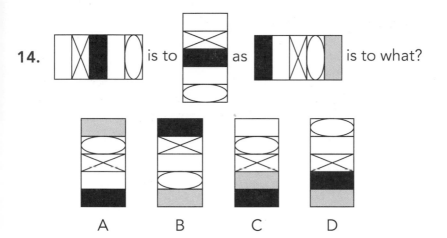 as 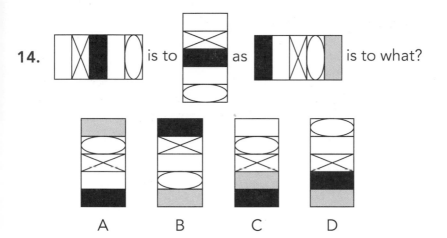 is to what?

A   B   C   D

15. How many rectangles of all sizes are there in this diagram? (Squares count as rectangles.)

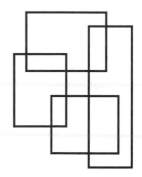

ANSWERS 19

1. 3. C

   Treat the letters as their numerical positions in the alphabet. $(7 + \sqrt{25}) \div 4 = (7 + 5) \div 4 = 12 \div 4 = 3$, which is C, since C is the 3rd letter of the alphabet.

2. 200 grams

   2Y + the mug weighs 500. Y + the mug weighs 350. Subtracting, Y by itself weighs 150. Therefore the mug weighs 350 – 150 = 200.

3. TORONTO

4. SMALL, MEDIUM, LARGE

5. BARREL and ARABLE

   Fill in an A and read counterclockwise from it to spell ARABLE. Fill in an R and read clockwise from the B to spell BARREL.

6. HOCKEY, becoming JOCKEY

7. NCE

The sequence consists of the last three letters of the words in the question "wHAT, tripLET, finisHES, tHIS, unusUAL, sequeNCE?"

8. 12

Reading across, the letters spell "FIXED SUM." The fixed sum they refer to is the sum of each letter's position in the alphabet and the number in the corresponding column. The fixed sum is 25, since for 19 and F, F = 6 and 19 + 6 = 25. Similarly, for I and 16, I = 9 and 9 + 16 = 25. All the vertical sums total 25. Since M is the 13th letter of the alphabet and 13 + 12 = 25, the number that should appear below the M is 12.

9. ROMANTIC is the solution that we hope you'll "love." Since CORN = 8215, we have C = 8, O = 2, R = 1, and N = 5. Since ONION = 25725, we have I = 7. Since TOMATO = 623462, we have T = 6, M = 3, and A = 4. Putting these values in numerical order gives:

R O M A N T I C
1 2 3 4 5 6 7 8

10. B A E F D C

I visit F fourth, so the sequence looks like this:
_ _ _ F _ _. A and E must be visited next to each other, and since A is before D, E must be before D, too. D isn't before F because, if it were, B, A, and E would have to be before F, too, and there are only three visits, not four, in front of F. So D is after F, but not in the last spot: _ _ _ F D _. Since B, A, and E are all before D, they are in the first three spots, in that order: B A E F D _. The last person to be visited is C.

11. RABBI, RABBIT

12. B. PARK

They all form new words when the letter A is placed at the end. The words formed are PASTA, WHOA, TEMPERA, AREA, CHINA, DRAMA, and PARKA.

13. CBAD

Remove the first and last letters of the objects in the top row to make a word in the bottom row. ORANGE matches with RANG, BURGER with URGE, TWENTY with WENT, and BEAVER with EAVE.

14. D

Although it seems as if the diagram is merely rotating 90° clockwise, none of the answers fits this pattern. What else could be happening? Well, those two blank rectangles in the initial pattern could switch places without a noticeable difference! So the pattern is: switch the first and fourth rectangles, and then rotate 90° clockwise.

15. 10

Here is a list using the labeled diagram. One piece: B, C, E, G, J. Two pieces: GH (this is the one most people miss). Three pieces: ABC, BDG, CFJ, GHJ. That makes 10 rectangles total.

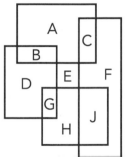

TEST 20

1. What is the last term in this five-term sequence?

   115B, 1630I, 3145N, 4660G, _____

2. Which of A, B, C, or D has the unusual property shared by the six words in the first column?

DAMN	A. REMIX
SMELL	B. SMEAR
STEM	C. FEMUR
MARBLE	D. MELON
FLAMED	
REMIND	

3. The same four letters are lacking from these two words, but not in the same order. If you rearrange these missing letters, they form a four-letter word. What's this four-letter word?

N E ___ ___ ___ ___ C E

B ___ ___ ___ ___ A S H

4. Insert a six-letter animal, one letter per square, across the top row of this grid so that six common four-letter words are formed reading down.

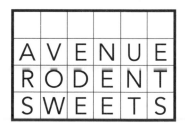

A	V	E	N	U	E
R	O	D	E	N	T
S	W	E	E	T	S

5. We've removed all of the vowels from a familiar saying and closed up the spaces. What saying is it?

L L S F R N L V N D W R

6. What eight-letter word meaning "took a plane" can be made from only letters in the first eleven positions of the alphabet, with no repeats?

A   B   C   D   E   F   G   H   I   J   K

7. **B R I** G R O **D** O **M E** is "bride" and "groom" interwoven. Both words keep their correct order from left to right. What two "this and that" words are interwoven here?

W O L I D S E E R R

8. Look closely. Which is the odd one out?

MARJORAM
REVOLVER
LACKADAISICAL
CINEMATIC
DETONATED
SCIOPTICS
FOOLPROOF

9. What two words beginning with CA mean "waterfall"?

CA_____   CA_____

10. Which word comes next? Choose from words A to E below.

refusal, coming, rail, estate, column, sense, _____

    A. light
    B. officer
    C. carpet
    D. coffee
    E. heaven

11. What four-letter dog becomes a much larger animal when you remove its second letter?

12. What four-letter topic word soundly encompasses the three words below? We've given you the third letter of the topic.

TOWS
SOULS
HEALS

Topic: ___ ___ A ___

13. What musical instrument can be represented by PAPERER in a cryptogram?

14. Arrange the five pictures below to form a chain in which each consecutive pair forms a compound word or two-word phrase, such as FLOWER BED ROOM SERVICE (flower bed, bedroom, room service). We've placed a HOUSE in the third spot to get you started.

A

B

C

D

E

15. Each of the six letters stands for a different from from 1 through 9. Using the three clues below, can you deduce the number represented by each letter?

A	B	C
D	E	F

The total of each row across is 15.
   All three columns down have the same total.
   The value of A + D + E is 18.
   The value of B + F is 6.

ANSWERS 20

1. 61750

   These are the number ranges associated with the letters in the game BINGO. 1–15 is B, 16–30 is I, 31–45 is N, 46–60 is G, and 61–75 is O.

2. B. SMEAR

   Each word in the list can have its M inverted to make a W and still form a word. The words are DAWN, SWELL, STEW, WARBLE, FLAWED, REWIND. Of the choices listed, only SMEAR will make a new word with a flipped M: SWEAR. (You might remember this trick from Test 5, Question 8.)

3. LACK

   The two words with parts lacking are NECKLACE and BACKLASH.

4.

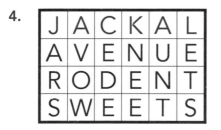

J	A	C	K	A	L
A	V	E	N	U	E
R	O	D	E	N	T
S	W	E	E	T	S

5. All's fair in love and war

6. HIJACKED

7. OLDER and WISER

8. CINEMATIC
The three-letter chunk at the beginning of each word appears backward at the end of each word in every case except for CINEMATIC. For example, MARJORAM begins with MAR and ends with its reversal, RAM.

9. CASCADE and CATARACT

10. E. heaven
    The words in the series can all be preceded by
    the corresponding ordinal numbers: FIRST refusal,
    SECOND coming, THIRD rail, FOURTH estate, FIFTH
    column, SIXTH sense, SEVENTH heaven.

11. CHOW (becoming COW)

12. FEAT
    The words given are homophones of TOES, SOLES,
    HEELS, so the topic is a homophone of FEET.

13. UKULELE
    The word UKULELE has the same letter-substitution
    pattern as PAPERER.

14. D B E C A
    The words and phrases are FAMILY TREE, TREE
    HOUSE, HOUSECOAT, COATTAIL, and TAILGATE.

15.

A 7	B 2	C 6
D 3	E 8	F 4

Since both rows total 15, the sum of all of the numbers in the grid is 30. Since all three columns have the same value, each column totals 10. So, in particular, A + D = 10. But we're told that A + D + E = 18, so E = 8. This means that B = 2, since the middle column totals 10. But we're told B + F = 6, so F = 4. Then C = 6 (column total 10), A = 7 (row total 15), and D = 3 (using row or column total).

TEST 21

1. In each line, find a four-letter word that follows the first word and precedes the second word to form two phrases (such as BEAR ___ TIGHT making "bearskin" and "skin-tight" when SKIN is entered.) The three words you supply, in order, will form a familiar phrase.

$$\begin{array}{ccc} \text{BIT} & \text{_____} & \text{COMPANY} \\ \text{RESPONSE} & \text{_____} & \text{CAPSULE} \\ \text{CLOCK} & \text{_____} & \text{BENCH} \end{array}$$

2. Change one letter in each word to form a common saying.

MOVE AS BLINK

3. Which of A, B, or C belongs with the two items on the top line?

↑UNORTHODOX   →SEA STAR   _____

    A. ↓UNOPENED
    B. ←AWESTRUCK
    C. ↓INOPERATIVE

4. Some blocks are piled in the corner of a room, creating this pattern. How many blocks are used in all?

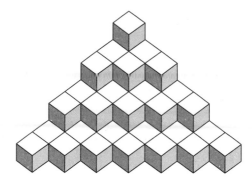

5. Find six different (but related) words to follow these words. If you do it correctly, the answers will come out in alphabetical order.

SPRING _____
LEGAL _____
SILLY _____
NIGHT _____
STOOL _____
CULTURE _____

6. Two circles, a triangle, and a rectangle (of sizes of your choosing) are drawn on a piece of paper. What is the maximum possible number of points of intersection of these four figures? (Assume that the number of points of intersection is not infinite. In other words, the triangle doesn't share an edge with the rectangle, and the two circles do not overlap completely.)

7. Solve this nsal crossword.

1	2	3	4
5			
6			
7			

ACROSS
1. One who deldes
5. Gets all fzzy
6. nsharpened
7. Head-and-sholders
   sclptres

DOWN
1. proar
2. Rminates (over)
3. Main impact, as of a
   pnch
4. Sdden blasts of wind

8. What identical name could you give to a truant, a stone thrower, a schoolgirl on a playground, or a ship's handler?

9. Insert a four-letter word that completes the
    first word and starts the second, like DIVE in
    EN(___ ___ ___ ___)RT making ENDIVE and
    DIVERT.

    RES (___ ___ ___ ___) EROUS

10. Pair up these 14 words, always taking one from
    Column 1 and one from Column 2, to create 7
    eight-letter words. Something tricky is going on
    here, though, so be careful!

Column 1	Column 2
ATOP	BLED
ACED	DENT
BIRD	HOES
CURT	KING
EELS	LASS
GYPS	PIER
SMUG	TOES

11. Which of A, B, C, or D belongs with the five sets of letters listed on the left?

KGI   A. SOQ
HDF   B. TWY
NJL   C. OKN
EAC   D. VSU
ZVX

12. Place the numbers 1, 2, 3, 4, 5, 6, 7 in the spaces of this diagram so that the sum of the numbers in each circle totals nine. (Hint: Start by making a list of all of the combinations that add to 9.)

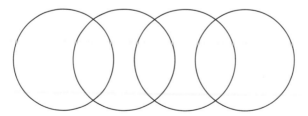

13. What three-letter word can go into all six blanks to form six new words?

___ ___ ___ ROT	___ ___ ___ VENUS
___ ___ ___ AMOUNT	___ ___ ___ LANCE
___ ___ ___ SNIP	___ ___ ___ TYING

14. Add the same letter to each four-letter word, and rearrange the letters to spell a five-letter word. Write the words in the corresponding row of the diagram, one letter per square. The added letter must always fall in the shaded square.

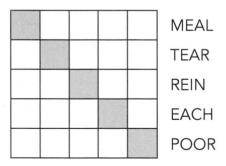

MEAL

TEAR

REIN

EACH

POOR

15. The six numbered images are transparencies.
Three of them, when stacked on top of each other
without rotating them, can form the pattern below.
Which three?

1

2

3

4

5

6

1. PART-TIME WORK

   PART makes the phrases "bit part" and "(to) part company." TIME makes "response time" and "time capsule." WORK makes the words "clockwork" and "workbench."

2. LOVE IS BLIND

3. B

   In each of the three, a direction follows the first letter, and the arrow points in that direction: uNORTHodox, sEA STar, aWESTruck. The two wrong answers both tell you "NOPE"!

4. 50

   Counting the blocks in the layers from bottom to top, we have 28 + 15 + 6 + 1.

5. CHICKEN, EAGLE, GOOSE, OWL, PIGEON, VULTURE
The familiar phrases are "spring chicken," "legal eagle," "silly goose," "night owl," "stool pigeon," and "culture vulture."

6. 36
The two circles can intersect each other at 2 points. Each circle can intersect the rectangle at 8 points, making 16 points. The triangle can intersect each circle at 6 points, making 12 points. The triangle can intersect the rectangle at 6 points. Thus the maximum number of intersections is 2 + 16 + 12 + 6 = 36.

7. The clues suggest leaving out all of the U's. All of the answers to the clues contain only the vowel U. The words across are HUMBUG, BLURS, BLUNT, and BUSTS. The words down are HUBBUB, MULLS, BRUNT, and GUSTS.

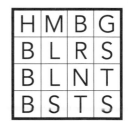

8. SKIPPER

9. POND

The words formed are RESPOND and PONDEROUS.

10. POTATOES, DECADENT, DRIBBLED, TRUCKING, SLEEPIER, SPYGLASS, GUMSHOES

The words in Column 1 must be turned backward before they are matched to the words in Column 2. For example, ATOP backward is POTA, and adding POTA to TOES makes POTATOES.

11. A

Each three-letter chunk consists of a letter with two related letters in front of it. The pattern is (letter + 2)(letter – 2)(letter). Since S is two after Q and O is two before Q, the group SOQ fits the pattern.

12. Either this answer, or its reverse:

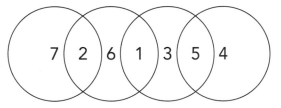

How is it solved? Well, first make the list of possible combinations. Pairs that add to nine are (2, 7), (3, 6), and (4, 5). Triples that add to nine are (1, 2, 6), (1, 3, 5), and (2, 3, 4). Since 7 appears only in a pair, you know that it must be at one of the two ends. The 2 goes beside it. Now consider the shaded area (shown at right). This is the overlap of two triples. The only

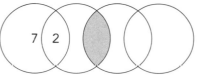

numbers that appear in two different triples are 1, 2, and 3, but we've already used the 2. So this central spot must contain 1 or 3. The 3 leads nowhere (try it), while the 1 yields the solution.

13. PAR
    The words formed are PARROT, PARVENUS, PARAMOUNT, PARLANCE, PARSNIP, and PARTYING.

14. FLAME, AFTER, INFER, CHAFE, PROOF
    The letter added is F.

15. 2, 4, 5

1. In the following sequence, each number from 1 to 8 occurs twice, with each number indicating how many places after the first occurrence of that number is the second occurrence of that number:

    8 6 4 2 7 2 4 6 8 3 5 7 3 1 1 5

    For example, the second 6 is six places after the first 6. Construct a 10-digit sequence with the same property, using the numbers from 1 to 5 twice.

2. Among 30 ice cream cones with either chocolate or vanilla ice cream on either a plain or sugar cone, 14 have sugar cones, 19 have vanilla ice cream, and 2 have chocolate ice cream on a plain cone. How many have vanilla ice cream on a sugar cone?

3. Match each picture in the top row with a picture in the bottom row by writing letters in the blanks.

A   B   C   D   E

___   ___   ___   ___   ___

4. What is the next term in this sequence?

I1   II2   III3   IV3   V2   VI3   VII4   VIII5   IX3   ___

5. WH1T 3T2M 5S2D F4R 3N4C5L1T34NS 3S 1LS4 1 W4RD M21N3NG "1NN46"?

6. Change each three-letter group into a seven-letter word or phrase by putting the same pair of letters before and after. Definitions appear, in no particular order, in the second column. If you complete all four groups correctly, the pairs of letters, reading down, form an eight-letter bonus word whose definition also appears in the list.

____ C A P ____	Dance music
____ R I O ____	Gets away
____ S C A ____	Increase in intensity
____ R M I ____	Household pest
Bonus word: _____	Milan opera house: 2 wds.

7. What three-letter word can fill all four blanks to create four new words?

MEN ___ ___ ___   SURF ___ ___ ___

GRIM ___ ___ ___   PAL ___ ___ ___

8. If "L B at F" means "Life begins at forty," then what proverb is this?

W the C A, the M W P.

9. Which of A, B, C, or D has the unusual property shared by the six words listed?

CANTATA
SLYLY
CATERER
BANANA
WHIRLIGIG
BROUHAHA

A. HOBNOB
B. PARALLEL
C. KIMONO
D. CRISIS

10. What famous island can be inserted into both letter groups to form two new words?

WHERROW   KISA

11. Below are two word squares with two sets of clues. In each square, the same words read across and down. Each clue number is followed by two different clues to two different answers. The challenge is to figure out which answer goes into which grid. We've filled in the upper left corners of each grid for you.

F				

1
2
3
4
5

S				

1. Out of touch with reality
   Cuba's Castro
2. One from Baghdad
   Italian pie
3. Piece of info
   Quetzalcoatl worshipper
4. From Prague
   Outfit
5. Walks lamely
   Billionaire's boat

12. Anagram the red word in this sentence to make a word that fits in the blank.

The school bus driver was arrested for having _____ on all four wheels of the bus.

13. What seven-letter tree can be made from only the letters in the odd-numbered positions in the alphabet? Here are the possible letters:

A C E G I K M O Q S U W Y

14. If you overlap the last letter of HEAT with the first letter of THEN, you get the word HEATHEN. What seven-letter word meaning "sincere" do you get by similarly overlapping a word meaning "deserve" with a word meaning "cardinal's home"?

15. Which of A, B, or C comes next in this sequence?

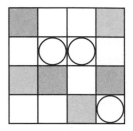 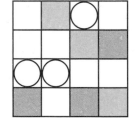 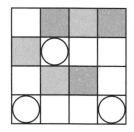

A	B	C

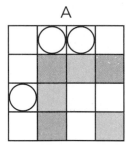 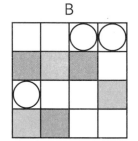 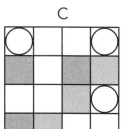

1. There are 10 possible solutions. Each is the reverse of the one across from it.

    1 1 3 4 5 5 3 2 4 2 5   5 2 4 2 3 5 4 3 1 1
    1 1 5 2 4 2 3 5 4 3   3 4 5 3 2 4 2 5 1 1
    4 1 1 5 4 2 3 2 5 3   3 5 2 3 2 4 5 1 1 4
    5 1 1 3 4 5 3 2 4 2   2 4 2 3 5 4 3 1 1 5
    4 5 1 1 4 3 5 2 3 2   2 3 2 5 3 4 1 1 5 4

2. 5

    Organize the data into a chart like the one at right. (The given information is written in black.) Since there are 30 ice cream cones in all, we can work out the totals for the plain-cone row (30 − 14 = 16) and for the chocolate column (30 − 19 − 11), then use these values to complete the chart with the new information shown in red.

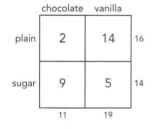

	chocolate	vanilla	
plain	2	14	16
sugar	9	5	14
	11	19	

3. BEDAC

The pictures combine to form familiar words and phrases (birdhouse, flowerbed, firefly, peanut butter, and mountain lion).

4. X2

These are the Roman numerals followed by the number of pencil strokes needed to make each one.

5. NEEDLE (or N22DL2)

The letters A, E, I, O, U, Y have been replaced with the numbers 1, 2, 3, 4, 5, 6, respectively. The sentence, when decoded, reads: "What item used for inoculations is also a word meaning 'annoy'?"

6. ESCAPES (gets away)
CARIOCA (dance music)
LA SCALA (Milan opera house)
TERMITE (household pest)
Bonus word: ESCALATE (increase in intensity)

7. ACE

The words are MENACE, GRIMACE, SURFACE, and PALACE.

8. When the cat's away, the mice will play.

9. D. CRISIS
All of the words have a repeated pair of letters at the end (such as HA in brouHAHA, or IS in crISIS.)

10. ELBA
The words are wheELBArrow and kiELBAsa (Polish sausage). Elba, an island off the west coast of Italy, was the site of Napoleon's first exile.

11.

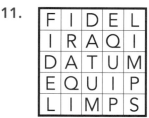

1
2
3
4
5

12. RETREADS

13. SEQUOIA

14. EARNEST

    The overlapping words are EARN and NEST.

15. B

    Every square in the grid shifts one square down and one square to the left at each step. The grid wraps around; that is, squares that disappear off the left side of the grid reappear on the right and squares that disappear off the bottom of the grid reappear on the top.